D1002506

## the
# *Healing Wisdom*
## *of* BIRDS

## About the Author

Lesley Morrison has explored the realms of mythology, animal symbolism, and spiritual traditions for many years, expanding her knowledge of multicultural practices and how they integrate the human experience. She studied anthropology and psychology at Athabasca University, and has worked closely with several Native American healers and medicine women. She is actively involved in wildlife rehabilitation, particularly where birds are involved, and hopes to raise awareness about the growing dangers birds face in the modern world.

Lesley currently resides on Vancouver Island with her daughter where she continues to explore the wonders of nature every day.

# Lesley Morrison

The
Healing Wisdom
of BIRDS

An
Everyday
Guide to Their
Spiritual Songs
& Symbolism

Llewellyn Publications
Woodbury, Minnesota

*The Healing Wisdom of Birds: An Everyday Guide to Their Spiritual Songs & Symbolism*
© 2011 by Lesley Morrison. All rights reserved. No part of this book may be used or reproduced in any manner whatsoever, including Internet usage, without written permission from Llewellyn Publications, except in the case of brief quotations embodied in critical articles and reviews.

Cover art and interior illustrations © by Kate Birch
Cover design by Ellen Lawson
Editing by Connie Hill

Llewellyn Publications is a registered trademark of Llewellyn Worldwide Ltd.

ISBN 978-0-7387-1882-8

Llewellyn Worldwide Ltd. does not participate in, endorse, or have any authority or responsibility concerning private business transactions between our authors and the public.
    All mail addressed to the author is forwarded, but the publisher cannot, unless specifically instructed by the author, give out an address or phone number.
    Any Internet references contained in this work are current at publication time, but the publisher cannot guarantee that a specific location will continue to be maintained. Please refer to the publisher's website for links to authors' websites and other sources.

Llewellyn Publications
A Division of Llewellyn Worldwide Ltd.
2143 Wooddale Drive
Woodbury, MN 55125-2989

Printed in the United States of America

# Contents

*For Kailey, Rachael, Hunter,*
*Mom & Dad*

Introduction

*Zeus won't in a hurry the sceptre restore to the*
*Woodpecker tapping the oak.*
*In times prehistoric 'tis easily proved,*
*by evidence weighty and ample,*
*That birds and not gods were the*
*rulers of men, and the lords of the world.*

—ARISTOPHANES, *THE BIRDS*[1]

When I first undertook this project, many people asked me why I felt compelled to write a whole book about birds. My answer? I was haunted, day and night, until I did. The universe has a funny way of making its advice known, and after many challenging encounters and rescues with feathered creatures I finally got the message. I became alerted to the silent mission before me, and was compelled by an unyielding insistence to pay closer attention to birds and their world. So I remained haunted until the final manuscript was complete.

The process of creating this book was a strange combination of joy, sadness, intrigue, and wonder. I read many books about birds that made me cry—forcing me to learn both the tragedies and celebrations of birds over time in

---

1. Written in 414 BCE, *The Birds* was wildly comical in its day and has remained one of the classics of ancient Greek comedy.

their relationships with the complex world of humans. People and birds have had a long relationship, but somewhere in time a very important philosophy was lost to the insatiable, three-faceted monster we call civilization, advancement, and modernization. Most people do not know how something as tangible as women's fashion nearly destroyed an abundant population of cranes in the early part of the twentieth century. Hundreds of thousands of birds were killed for their feathers, and cranes nearly became extinct for the sake of fashionable ladies' hats.

So what went wrong in the human soul to allow such a devastating betrayal of life? Once you have read this book, you too will call for an answer. I will not dwell so much on the tragedies of birds in this book, but will invite you to a celebration of their impact on humanity and the wonder they once brought to the human heart and soul. I like to consider it a voice in a dark wilderness for the avian world who have very little time on their side.

The journey begins with the Bird goddess image, and its continuity throughout many prominent cultures in the world. Then we will dive into the Cosmic Egg, a worldwide mythology that explains the beginning of the world. From there we explore birds and feathers in shamanism and magic, finally taking a detailed look at dozens of specific birds and their historical and spiritual attributes.

You will find that an invisible but undeniable thread exists in the sphere of bird symbolism connecting the past with the present. It is a deep exploration, and also an invitation into the archetypal world of the winged ones. It will show you, the reader and bird lover, the hows and whys of their importance in the world as spiritual guides, omens, helpers, and unrivaled creatures of the sky. I hope this book inspires you to a deeper appreciation of birds and encourages greater conservation efforts on your part. At the end of the book I have included a list of worldwide organizations that are devoted to the protection and rehabilitation of birds, as well as everyday things we can all do to help our feathered friends enjoy a full and happy life.

1

The Bird
Goddess

The bird goddess image seemed the most fitting way to begin a study of bird symbolism. It is an enduring archetype in mythology, and one that helped shape many tales and superstitions about birds that we still see today. When I began my research I traced the images of goddesses around the world. Not surprisingly, many of them appeared with birds, as birds, or with some attribute of a feathered creature. The centuries were filled with wild and glorious winged beings acting as alter egos for the goddesses of old. There was Athena, the famous patron goddess of the Greek world, and her beloved companion owl, and Saraswati, the East Indian goddess of knowledge, pulled in her chariot by large white swans. These images reveal an ancient mystery between birds and divine beings that lingered for centuries in the tales of every culture.

And so the mystery unfolded. Beginning two million years ago in the Paleolithic Era, people could see the connections between bird and spirit. The ancient caves were adorned with birdlike figures—as a form of art, the expression of a shamanic vision, or as some menacing form of early worship unfamiliar to the modern eye. These images are among the most enduring in world mythology, evolving throughout time from one deity to another, but always merging with the same primal nature of the mother figure. Birds repeatedly overshadow other forms of animals as symbols of the iconic image called the Great Mother Goddess. [2]

This cultural reverence for birds would have made better sense to the prescientific ages, where anything nonhuman would have been mysterious and fascinating. Even the political and cultural sophistication of Imperial Rome relied on birds for oracular advice. The disappearance and reappearance of migrating birds, for one thing, would have been unexplainable, and tracking the migration patterns of birds would have been an unimaginable feat in the ancient world. From these gaps in scientific knowledge arose a world of superstitions and myths, many of them focusing on a powerful bird deity.

Many of the world's beliefs about birds actually arose from the goddess or god they attended in mythological tales, feats, and spiritual quests. Most are familiar with the "wise old owl," an archetype that descended from Athena, the Greek goddess of wisdom. The ill-omened crow, earning a bad reputation over the years, assisted the Irish goddess Morrigan in devouring the dead on the battlefield. Perusing the ancient mythologies allows our somewhat disconnected modern mindset to grasp something universal— something that puts all the pieces back together again.

In Neolithic times, the Bird goddess was also seen as the bringer of the life-giving rains. This expression evolved much later into myths and superstitions about birds and their abilities to predict and control the weather. From these

---

2. The Mother Goddess was representative of female fertility, and was regarded as the source of life and death. Goddess worship predated patriarchal religions by thousands of years.

early beliefs descends the multicultural phenomena of augury, or divination by the observation of birds, which will be explored in greater detail later on.

In Bronze Age art (3300–1200 BCE), and in representations much later on, artists would portray ducks as ships, and often showed them pulling vehicles bearing the goddess herself. This is one of my favorite motifs, reaffirming the bird as a sort of guide on the spiritual journey, similar to the shamanic vision quest. Very early on, the bird became a companion of the goddess image and an aid to her otherworldly powers. Many more images of birds and the Mother Goddess appear during the Bronze Age, like the Cosmic Egg—from which the entire universe came forth—and how it was laid by the cosmic mother bird. The cracking open of this egg was the beginning of both time and space in many world mythologies (the Cosmic Egg motif is discussed in greater detail in the next chapter). This is the most explicit example of the bird as an image of fertility through its connection with this primordial giver of life.

Another fascinating clue to the bird/goddess mystery was unearthed in the Orkney Islands, where thirty-five sea eagles were found entombed with human skeletons. Perhaps this indicates the role of birds as companions, or even vehicles, to the otherworld after a person's death. This is just another of those tell-tale signs revealing a lost, ancient connection between birds and the goddess as an image of death and regeneration.

Many myths around the world describe a goddess who brings messages to the human world in the guise of birds. Not just an ancient idea, this is a concept that has been incorporated everywhere, even today in modern pagan traditions. The bird was once the most sacred of animals to pagan worshipers, and among the primary totemic allies in many shamanic cultures as well. In early Greek culture, the poet Homer wrote that the goddess was able to change into a bird.[3]

Such spiritually empowering images have provided a universal commonality—telling a fascinating story of how early humans viewed themselves within this great unknown cosmos. Although the human species is not very old compared to many others, it certainly grasped the importance of the natural world, particularly animals and birds, right from the start. Had the human spirit not wandered so far from this insightful existence, I imagine the world would be a totally different place right now.

## The Bird Goddesses: A Closer Look

The following goddesses have had enduring associations with birds throughout history, and are often directly descended from the goddess images of Neolithic times. Use these descriptions as starting points for your own exploration of bird goddesses.

### Inanna: Divine Lady Owl

A complex goddess image, Inanna carries a very old bird connection. She was the beloved Babylonian Queen of Heaven, and myths portrayed her as a Great Mother Goddess figure

---

3. Homer's *Iliad* makes references to the goddess Athena taking the form of a bird as she comes to the aid of the warriors in battle.

from around the third millennium BCE. Inanna was seemingly a goddess of contradiction, being a deity of both love and war, and was always depicted with multiple aspects. She was a sky goddess, and not surprisingly, often shown accompanied by a bird. Her principal bird images, or bird companions, were the dove, the owl, and the swallow, giving her a distinctive cultural thread to the Neolithic Bird goddess images of older times.

It is fitting, however, to find the owl as Inanna's strongest bird epiphany, as both shared spiritual connections to death and its inevitable regeneration. The goddess was also often depicted with the death-dealing talons of an owl indicating her connection to the netherworld. Her mythological tales boasting a descent into the underworld enhances her connection to this great bird, who is historically considered an omen of death. Interestingly, the Sumerian word for owl is *Ninna,* and the name *Nin-ninna,* given to the goddess in her owl form, meant *Divine Lady Owl.* Like a great winged bird, Inanna was considered a ruler of the skies and the heavens.

## Freya: Goddess of the Feathered Cloak

Freya, or Frejya, was an intriguing goddess figure, and one of my favorite mythological deities, with attributes that seem to parallel those in ancient shamanic traditions. She was said to possess a marvelous cloak of falcon feathers that allowed her to transform into any kind of bird. This shape-shifting ability was of course an integral aspect of early shamanic practices. This cloak was called *Valshamr,* meaning "hawk's plumage," "falcon-skin," or "falcon-feathered cloak." Freya was also known as a great seer, tying together nicely the hawk's keen vision and the magical ability of prophetic vision. In many instances throughout mythology, the goddess and the shaman utilize the power of birds and their feathers to perform magical acts.

### Athena: The Bright-Eyed Owl Goddess

Athena, the owl-eyed, or owl-faced goddess of war and wisdom, was patron goddess of skilled crafts; the owl, the wisest of birds, was one of her special symbols. Athena was the preeminent goddess of the ancient Grecian City of Athens, but still more ancient is her association with the diver-bird and the owl. On a Corinthian vase dating back to the sixth century BCE, Athena is depicted in her chariot while behind her, perched on a horse, is a woman-headed bird. This archaic image reveals Athena's descent from the earlier Neolithic bird goddess images, and helps us trace an obvious iconic evolution. Her origins from an earlier owl goddess, who could take the form of both owl and human, appear in Homer's epic poem the *Odyssey*, where the goddess typically disappears in a rush of wings or in the form of a fellow bird of prey. If Athena did in fact descend from the owl-goddess of much earlier times, her role as wisdom-goddess of ancient Greece would have stemmed from the role of the owl-goddess, as the intense staring eyes of the owl made it an emblem of bright wisdom and intelligence.

### Aphrodite: Lady of Love

One of the world's most well-known goddesses, the Greek Aphrodite—or Roman Venus—shares a similar symbolism with the ancient dove goddess of Crete. Aphrodite reveals her descent from the iconic bird goddess through her many bird forms, or epiphanies, especially that of the white dove, said to be the original form of the bird goddess. Aphrodite's other companion birds included the swan and the goose, and she is often shown riding elegantly through the skies upon these majestic birds. This is another example of the evolution of archetypal imagery throughout differing cultural practices. The whiteness of the swan alludes to Aphrodite's purity and dignity, and throughout the Bronze Age this bird was often depicted as her alternate form. The swan's association with love and beauty comes from the ancient image of being the bird companion of the goddess of love.

### Artemis: Goddess of the Wild

The ancient Greek goddess Artemis reigned over the wilderness, and thus all of the creatures who dwell within it. She was the patron goddess of the hunt, and represented the balance between being compassionate toward animals, and hunting them for nutritional and survival needs. Although Artemis is usually depicted with the deer, she is also a bird goddess, and has been seen with the guinea fowl and the buzzard. As a bird goddess, Artemis is the most closely connected to the ancient bird and stick motif—a symbolism that dates back to the cave paintings of the Paleolithic. The image is often identified with the tree of the goddess, and is a strong shamanic symbol around the world. Amulets of the solar hawk and the bird on a pole have all been found in profusion with her.

## Saraswati: The Divine Swan Maiden

Saraswati is the Hindu goddess of knowledge, and has been eloquently depicted over the centuries with her wonderful bird companions. She is traditionally shown with two different birds, the peacock and the swan, depending upon the philosophical tradition in which you explore. When the two forms are shown together, they are thought to represent the two forms of knowledge: the mundane (material) and the transcendent (spiritual). The swan is considered a symbol of transcendence and perfection within Indian mythology, and as the companion of Saraswati, the higher quality of mind that comes from the attainment of knowledge. There is also a belief that the swan will choose to drink pure milk over milk mixed with water. As a companion and carrier of the goddess of wisdom, this symbolizes the need to discriminate between right and wrong actions, and to let knowledge guide our actions.

## Lakshmi: Goddess of Fortune

Another owl-goddess, Lakshmi was worshipped in early times primarily as an earth deity. In the *Ramayana* [4] she is a beautiful goddess of fortune and prosperity and "one of the treasures born of the churning of the sea of milk." Lakshmi's primary bird vehicle is the owl. I find this an interesting connection because the owl is not often attributed to fortune and prosperity (in fact, it is usually the opposite), but in this instance seems fitting as Lakshmi ensures agri-

---

4. The *Ramayana* is an ancient Sanskrit epic, dating to around 750–500 BCE, and is attributed to the Hindu sage Valmiki.

cultural prosperity and the owl feeds upon crop-destroying rodents.

## Oshun: Goddess of Beauty and Life

Many of the world's most vivid myths come to us from Africa, and one of its primary deities, Oshun, embodies the bold, primitive beauty of the goddess figure. Her name comes from the Oshun river in Nigeria, and she is the Yoruba Orisha (deity) of the sweet rivers that sustain life. She rules over love, intimacy, wealth, beauty, and dance. Oshun represents the colors of the peacock and the parrot, her two primary bird companions, who both radiate beauty and joy in their colorful plumage. Like these birds, beauty belongs to Oshun, and reminds us of our ability to create beauty for its own sake. The peacock feather fan of Oshun is used by initiates to cleanse and remove obstructions

## Morrigan: Lady of the Crows

Many of the goddesses in Celtic tradition, particularly the more aggressive goddesses presiding over war and death, were heavily associated with the crow and raven. These birds were especially sacred to Morrigan, the red-haired battle goddess of the Tuatha De Danaan. The Morrigan gives warning of coming battles, urges on her chosen side, and finally takes the form of a crow or raven to feed upon the slain. In time, these birds' appearances during and after battle gave them the reputation of harbingers of death and ill omens. Throughout European culture, crows and ravens were considered connected to the otherworld and the beings who resided there. Even today, they are looked upon with a hint of suspicion as the old mythologies linger in the human psyche.

### Lil–Lilith/Lilith: The Screech Owl

Lil-Lilith is an interesting bird/goddess connection, revealing the revamping of old pagan goddesses in the church after the rise of Christianity. Lilith was a Sumerian—Akkadian goddess whose name later appears in the Hebrew Old Testament. It has been assumed that Lilith's name may translate to *screech owl*, and that this old association with the bird of the underworld contributed to her sinful nature in the Bible. Lilith, like many early goddess images, has been stripped of her sacred nature by the biblical restoration of the pagan deities. Lilith was probably a goddess connected with the regenerative powers of death, accompanied by the owl as the bird who naturally rules death and the underworld.

### Isis & Nekhbet: Goddesses of the Nile

One of the better-known goddesses, Isis was the Egyptian deity of renewal and magic. As one of the guards of the Pharaoh's sarcophagus, she appeared in ancient Egyptian art as a great winged bird, often in the form of a falcon. When her husband Osiris was killed, the goddess manifested herself as the great Neolithic bird goddess, fanning her great wings to bring him back to life. Other than the falcon, she is often depicted as a kite, along with her sister Nephthys, or as a mighty vulture who frees the spirit by removing the flesh of the deceased. Having resurrected her husband, the vulture would appear as a fitting bird companion for Isis as the renewer of life after death.

Another Egyptian vulture goddess, Nekhbet became the national goddess and represented Upper Egypt. As one of the principal deities mentioned in the Pyramid Texts, she is depicted as a vulture protecting the Pharaoh as she hovers over him with outstretched wings, or as a female figure wearing a vulture skin on her head.

### Rhiannon: The Great Queen of Magic

In Celtic folklore, the beautiful and powerful goddess Rhiannon (meaning "Great Queen"), had strong associations with birds. She is often seen attended by three songbirds, usually shown as blackbirds, who could revive the dead and sing to weary heroes to lull them to sleep. The blackbirds were considered the doorkeepers to the underworld, and in *Mabinogion*,[5] the "Song of Branwen" recounts that these enchanting birds sing at a magical feast. Rhiannon's connection to birds highlights their magical gifts, and the centuries-old belief that bird song can bridge the human and spirit worlds.

### Some Bird Gods in World Mythology

Although largely associated with goddesses, birds were named companions of some male deities also. In most cases, the birds connected with gods were solar birds, like the hawk, falcon, and eagle.

**Re** was the preeminent solar deity of ancient Egypt, and was often represented anthropomorphically, but with the head of a hawk wearing a sun-disc headdress. Many of the ancient solar deities, in Egypt and elsewhere, were associated

---

5. Prose stories taken from medieval Welsh manuscripts, ca. 1100–1400.

with birds, particularly hawks, because of their ability to fly close to the sun.

**Horus** was the most important avian deity in the ancient religion of Egypt. The falcon, being symbolic of this god, seems to have been the most worshiped animal as representative of the greatest cosmic powers. Many Egyptian deities were portrayed as being either falcon-headed, or as having the wings of such a bird.

**Hraesvelgr**, a winter god, dresses in eagle plumes and directs the icy winds of Vasud to cause discomfort for mortals.

**Odin**, considered the chief god in Norse Paganism, is associated with wisdom, war, prophecy, magic, poetry, shape-shifting, victory, and the hunt. Odin's bird companions, Huginn (thought) and Muninn (memory) traveled the world and returned to Odin every night to give him news from the deeds of men. An old Norse prose about the raven pair reads: "The whole world wide, every day, fly Huginn and Muninn; I worry lest Huginn should fall in flight, yet more I fear for Muninn."[6]

6. From *Grimnismal*, a mythological poem of the Poetic Edda, ca. tenth century.

2

The Cosmic
Egg

*Long ago when all things animate and inanimate*
*were lost in one dreadful ocean there appeared*
*a large egg, source of the seed of all creatures.*[7]

I debated at first whether or not to include this chapter. But given the strong foundation of the bird goddess image and its impact on later bird deities, I felt that omitting an exploration of Cosmic Egg mythology would leave a gaping hole in the big picture of bird symbolism. The egg is one of those symbols that cannot be separated from bird mythology's rich past, and really seems like the beginning of a centuries-old reverence for avian life.

The fascination with the egg lies in its symbolism and its ability to capture a universal experience metaphorically. It is an archetype for birth and of all things in the process of becoming. The egg is often the beginning of the world, even the cosmos, in myths around the world, and is the preferred image for fertility and the womb of the mother goddess. The egg is a sacred image for those who seek to understand birds in a more spiritual way. Another enigma of the bird is its "double birth" from the egg, first from the mother, and

---

7. *Classical Hindu Mythology,* 32

finally freed from the confines of the shell itself. It is often said that birds are born twice, making their birth a powerful symbol of transformation akin to the butterfly.

After exploring many creation myths, the Cosmic Egg appears as a fascinating recurrence representing the seed that gives birth to the cosmos. As a universal symbol of new life and unlimited potential for creation, the Cosmic Egg contains the potentiality of all existence enclosed within its shell. In many egg creation myths, it is laid on the primal waters by a bird, sometimes in the guise of human a great bird goddess. Other times, the egg arises from empty void, an abyss, or a place of "non-being." At other times, however, the creation story sees the human race spring forth from the Cosmic Egg, or from a creator breaking out from the shell to commence the creation of the world.

Inseparable from egg symbolism and mythology is the bird goddess, which we explored in the last chapter. She is the original bringer of the egg and giver of new life. The Cosmic Egg image is the world's most enduring symbol for the eternal resurrection of life, and belongs to the mythology of the bird goddess because she is the *source* of life.

The egg is also closely related to water as the primordial element in which life gestates. The egg as an image of the womb was a favorite subject of the artists of Old Europe, and was carried on into later cultural traditions through cosmology. Images of the goddess, the egg, and the bird were inseparable in the Pagan world as being able to describe the fundamental forces of creative power.

From the Paleolithic Age onward, bird-shaped vases and egg-shaped jars were created as a resting place for souls awaiting rebirth. Ancient Egyptian mythology favored the egg image, and the generation of the Primal Egg was said to take place in what was known as "The Time of Non-Being." In the *Chandogya Upanishad*, a Hindu text, we see the same concept of "non-being" from which life sprang:

> In the beginning this world was merely non being... It developed. It turned into an egg. It lay for the period of a year. It was split asunder. One of the two eggshell parts became silver, one gold. That which was of silver is the earth. That which was of gold is the sky. What was the outer membrane is the mountains. What was the inner membrane is cloud and mist. What were the veins are the rivers. What was the fluid within is the ocean. Now, what was born there from is yonder sun.—*third Prapathaka—nineteenth khanda, 1–38*

The Cosmic Egg itself is usually described in mythology as being either gold or silver in color, representing the colors of the sun or the moon. In a Cosmic Egg myth from Tibet, a place where these types of stories abound, the water spirits from four original eggs produce the classes of people of the Tibetan social order. It is said that from the golden egg came those who are kings and from the turquoise egg came the servants. An iron egg brought forth the religious leaders, or holy men, and the social outcasts arose from a bronze egg.

In one of the most ancient egg creation myths from Tibet, there are five primordial elements that fuse to give form

---

8. Mid-first millennium BCE.

to two great eggs: hardness, fluidity, heat, motion, and space. One of the eggs, named Radiant, is composed of white light, while the other, named Black Misery, is made of darkness. The Radiant egg breaks open and becomes the scattered divinities (gods) of the universe. From Black Misery arises a being who brings forth ignorance, madness, pestilence, and demons into the world.

China's Cosmic Egg creation myth describes how the opposing principles of yin and yang came into being when the egg broke apart. In a myth from Borneo there are two creator spirits who take the form of birds, swooping down to the primal waters to gather up two eggs. One egg becomes the earth, and the other the sky. The Dogon people of West Africa have a Cosmic Egg mythology in which their creator god, Amma, assumes the form of the egg himself that contains the potentiality of the entire cosmos. In another version, the Creation deity places two sets of embryonic twins inside an egg who, upon leaving the shell, will join to create the world.

In the Greek Orphic myth, from the Orphic mystery cult of the seventh century BCE, *Time*, personified as Cronus, creates a silver egg that gives birth to Phanes, the androgynous creator of the universe.

In *The Birds*, first produced in Athens in the year 414 BCE, Aristophanes gives a whimsical account of the creation of the world through the voice of the birds themselves, describing the "First thing first born of the black-plumed Night" as "a wind-egg hatched in her [earth's] bosom."

In Tahitian myth, the creator deity himself lives inside the Cosmic Egg. When he finally breaks forth from the shell, he creates a counterpart of himself and together they undertake the great act of creation. The Finnish epic *Kalevala*[9] describes how the world came to be created from an egg laid by a diving duck. In Christian art, an ostrich egg symbolized the virgin birth—a belief stemming from Medieval times that ostrichs hatched of their own accord, and in Hindu mythology, Brahma was born of a golden egg. Egg symbolism was a powerful motif for connecting to the female powers of creation. It reminds us of the new life that comes after the long winter, and the promise of an eternal resurrection of the Great Earth Mother in the spring.

These myths empower the goddess image and recall a time in history when nature was a sacred source of power. Traces of egg mythology can still be found today, especially during the annual celebration of Easter, which was once a festival celebrating the return of Ostara, the fertility goddess who brought forth the spring.

9. An epic poem, compiled from Finnish folklore, nineteenth century.

# 3

# The Bird Shamans

*What it is to be man....oh, that we might learn...*
*from the lilies and the birds...let us consider seriously*
*the lilies and the birds as teachers...and imitate them.*

—SOREN KIERKEGAARD (FROM *THE LILIES OF THE FIELD*
AND *THE BIRDS OF THE AIR*, 1849)

When most people hear talk about the spiritual powers of animals, an immediate association with the shaman often comes to mind. Bird goddess and Cosmic Egg mythologies were great starting points for the study of bird symbolism. This chapter, however, opens up a whole new door of experiences and histories involving a much more primitive drive in the human spirit—that of merging with the natural world. To me, shamanism is the essence of such merging, and empowers individuals through the experience of other life forms.

Birds and shamans, like birds and goddesses, have enjoyed this symbiosis since the beginning of human culture, and the parallels between shamanic practices and early bird goddess worship are very clear and compelling. Both practices represent a bond that seems to transcend time and history, always finding a meaningful manifestation to a society as a whole. Bird goddesses, in particular, shared with the shaman the gift of shape-shifting through the use of feather cloaks or bird masks, and this ability to change into bird form runs through many of the world's greatest stories.

Many of you may wish to have that primordial relationship with birds that some shamans have, but are wondering to yourselves how exactly a shaman comes to "work" with a bird spirit. The answer? Very carefully. When a shaman wishes to call upon a bird spirit, he or she usually puts on a bird costume and becomes a vehicle for the collective spirit of all birds, or even just the collective spirit of their specific bird totem. Bird regalia has appeared as the most common device for conducting shamanic rituals (like feather cloaks, mock bird wings, beaks, etc.) because bird imagery and symbolism are consistent with the spirit work and soul activities of shamanism everywhere.[10] Imitating birds is an ancient ritual involving a tremendous output of energy and concentration. Watching a medicine man dance and flail his arms like a bird practically sums up the shamanic image for many people. That is what shamans do to connect with the infinite spirit of a bird ally or guardian—they always have and they always will.

It must be remembered that to the people of ancient times animals were perceived as relations and not as separate entities, as they are today. It was believed that animals closely resembled humans and could be imitated through certain rituals and performances—like dancing and flapping the arms like a bird. It was also believed that animals could appear in human form as well. The idea of shapeshifting into a bird to harness its powers was an important aspect of many bird mythologies and religions of the past.

---

10. Tom Cowan, *Fire in the Head* (New York: Harper Collins, 1993).

It was also commonly believed that humans were able to fly and commune freely with avian life. As the centuries passed, only the highly trained, or initiated, could achieve such a feat—such as witches, shamans, yogis, and wizards. This concept reveals the fundamental beliefs of ancient peoples regarding the close ties of humans with animal beings. After studying this viewpoint from the perspective of many religions and cultures, I find it hard to believe that modern humans have drifted so far from what was once an obvious and necessary perception. If we had never become separated from that primordial connection, the animal and bird populations would never have suffered the devastating effects of today's disenchanted human reality.

The shamanic identification with flying birds enables human beings in every part of the world to escape from earth and move through space and time like gods. Birds, shamanism, and the flight of the soul are entities that can never escape each other, and have been that way since the Paleolithic period. Cave paintings at Lascaux (France), for example, reveal an image of a shaman figure lying on his back, wearing a bird mask, and having claw-like fingers.

Birds are usually also symbolic of the shaman's ecstatic journeying when he leaves his body to contact spirits in the other worlds. Only the bird can fly above and beyond the earthly realm, thus reaching other planes of existence with effortless grace and purpose. Birds are representatives of spiritual attainment and are still highly sought after for their knowledge of the secret workings of the universe. Wings and feathers imply and impart the ability to fly, enabling the shaman to travel to the spirit realms. In some traditions, the bird is believed to be the main spirit protector of a shaman, guiding him or her through the unknown regions of the universe. Birds are also the helping spirit most frequently portrayed in Inuit sculpture and art, and are usually shown on the shaman's head (stemming from a belief that the soul resides at the top of the head).

The bird is a psychopomp—a conductor of souls to the spirit realm—and the mythology of the bird-soul is both extensive and ancient. The early Egyptians used a hiero-glyph of a bird with a human head to represent *ba,* or soul, and in this culture birds served as symbols for the soul as it flew away from the body at death. This association with the bird and the soul was incorporated into Roman culture also, where an eagle was released at the funeral of a Caesar to guide his soul to Olympus—the eternal home of the gods. The Iroquois, too, set a bird free at the death of a chief. Celt-ic mythology holds a special place for this tradition as the battle goddesses would shape-shift into crows or ravens at the time of a warrior's death to guide his soul to Valhalla—the celestial hall of those slain in battle.

In many cultures, through the induction of an ecstatic trance and the simulation of a bird's flight, it was presumed that the shaman was able to conduct souls to their rest-ing place. The Nascan Indians of Peru ingested hallucino-genic cactus to produce the illusion of flying. Through the learned art of impersonation, or shape shifting, the shaman becomes the bird figure. The principal aid for the shaman during these rituals is his costume.

Shamanism has a long history in Siberia, where it is be-lieved that every shaman has a bird of prey for a mother, and the medicine men are believed to be directly descended from the birds they impersonate. They must learn to speak the language of birds as a component of their personal shamanic power. The Samoyed and Altaians wear caps decorated with bird feathers, while the Tungas and Yenesei tribes still shape their coats to resemble the wings and tail of an owl. The Sakha shamans of both sexes in this culture are said to have been able to give birth. Beginning at puberty, a shaman's training entailed birthing a raven or a loon, which instantly flew away.

The Tarahumara Indians of northwest Mexico dance to the music of their shaman's song to invoke the favor of their deities. They say that the birds taught them to leap and fly, play and stomp, in worship of a transcendental being behind the veil of nature. In Central Asia, *divana* (mystics possessed by spirits) wore hats made of swan feathers, while the mountain-men of China are often depicted as feathered birds themselves. The Maori shamans of New Zealand also wear feathered outfits, primarily for ceremonial use and to promote authority and identity among their groups.

The emperors of the ancient Inca empire of Peru were said to have lived in glorious palaces and wore robes made of hummingbird feathers. Birds are still considered shamanic characters in South American culture today, particularly owls, hummingbirds, harpy eagles, and vultures. In some South American narrative tales, the primal sun god lives in a shelter composed of yellow and red macaw feathers, and has the power to light the world with the feathers of his magnificent crown. The remains of parrots, recovered from Pachacamac and other coastal sites in Peru, were sometimes carefully wrapped in a miniature mummy bundle, revealing their great spiritual significance to Peru's ancient peoples. In modern-day Brazil the Bororo keep live birds in their village. When a Bororo Indian's pet macaw dies, it is wrapped in a fiber mat and buried behind the house. These birds are sacred among this tribe as the favorite dwelling place of ancestral spirits. The Bororo also believe themselves to be macaws, and say they were turned into birds by one of their culture heroes.

In shamanic practices, some birds are especially valued for being representatives of several worlds simultaneously. The loon and the duck, for example, representing air, water, and earth (underwater) are guides par excellence among many groups, such as the Komi and Khantey peoples of Russia. These birds were given great status as the masters of multiple worlds—a feat only attributed to the shaman in primitive cultures. During trance journeys, the shaman often takes on the form of a diving bird, able to reach the underworld by diving down. This diving is significant from a shamanic viewpoint, as many ancient cultures believe that sick spirits are held in the water. The symbolic meaning of diver birds usually differs greatly from that of other water birds because the diving bird seems to disappear beneath the surface into the underwater realm of death. These birds are also considered to be guides through the processes of death and rebirth.

Much knowledge concerning shamanism and totemic animals has come from the Native tribes of North America, but still contains the same fundamental principles and practices found around the world. Among the Yokut peoples of California, certain totemic animals were symbols of functional roles in the tribe. For example, the eagle was the totem of the chief, the dove was the totem of both the chief's and the shaman's messenger, and the owl was the totem of the shaman himself. The person in charge of ritual dance had the raven as his totem, and the intermediary between the chief and the people was associated with the magpie.

Elites of the old Mississippian culture (a mound-building Native American culture that began around 800–1500 CE), assumed to be members of chiefly and/or military cults associated with the falcon, wore painstakingly embossed copper feathers as part of their elaborate costumes. To the Yup'ik Eskimos, the *tengmiarpak,* meaning "big-bird," was an important part of their oral tradition. Capable of human speech, they were believed to be humans themselves who transformed into giant eagles after putting on their bird skins. Yup'ik hunters would also wear bird-skin clothing and once wore bird-skin parkas during the hunt for their lightness and warmth. In the Cherokee tradition, certain diseases are diagnosed by doctors as due to birds—either revengeful bird ghosts, bird feathers within the house, or bird shadows falling upon the patient from overhead.

Although many ancient peoples killed birds for food and for the use of their feathers, they usually did so within a framework of respect and deep appreciation. Many ancient cultures would even consume bird parts in the belief that they could absorb the bird's "Mana" (a Polynesian term, Mana refers to a mysterious spiritual power concentrated in certain objects—in this case, the body parts of the birds), and thus make imitation of the bird easier to accomplish.

Not only symbols of freedom, expansiveness, and the flight of the spirit, birds are given high regard cross-culturally for their keen vision. This becomes very symbolic for the spiritual work of the shaman, who requires a greater degree of intuitive sight in order to penetrate the layers of the human soul for healing. In this respect, the bird becomes representative of alternate levels of awareness because it is able to view the world from multiple perspectives. Ancient legends from Ireland and England describe not only medicine men, but faeries as being able to shape shift into birds of prey, like vultures, or into crows and ravens. The wearing of feathers for shamanic purposes was also prominent in Celtic tradition. Irish folklore often describes the feathered cloaks of poets, known as a *tugan*. This integral part of their performance regalia is believed to have been made from the feathers of songbirds, an appropriate association due to the poets reputation as a singer who shared with birds the power to lull listeners into a dream-like state with his song.

## The Language of the Birds

Many people don't even realize that they hear birds commune with each other every day. Many probably even interrupt great bird meetings unaware of the fantastic events occurring above them in trees, on top of buildings, or gathered around a puddle on a hot afternoon. For me, watching birds convene is always a chance to earn an entirely new perspective of their intelligence and unique social structures. I remember my first encounter with a large group of ravens—so completely superior in their ability to laugh at life and simply observe the chaos around them. They had gathered around a pothole in a secluded alley that I walked through every day. I walked along, completely unaware of them, when I heard the oddest noise—like some weird alien gibberish. When I came around the corner, the birds were determined to stare me down. They were appalled! I felt like I had walked in on some ancient magical ritual, and I, the nosy outsider, had just ruined the whole thing. I begged their pardon and quickly left the scene.

I am determined they had been discussing the day's events and probably telling jokes about us and our silly, disrupting lifestyles—like the way we throw out piles of good food in the trash every week, or water our driveways, or walk around with cell phones pasted to our ears. Those ravens were actually *talking* in some old language not suitable for human ears—and perhaps for good reason. I, for one, don't think they would be saying too many nice things about our species, do you?

It is well documented now that every bird species has its own language, and I knew this. I had just never heard such a fantastic and magical example of their vocal expressions before. The language of birds indeed seems otherworldly. Quite simply, it is something we are not permitted to understand. There have been, however, a few initiated individuals who have learned this secret language. In spiritual and magical contexts, the *language of the birds* has been described for centuries as being a perfect, mystical, divine, or magical language used by birds to communicate with the initiated. The "initiated" usually refers to shamans or powerful magicians. Sometimes, however, they are alchemists, and sometimes poets (or bards in the older traditions). In Norse mythology, the power to understand the language of birds was a sign of great wisdom. Lutwack explains how "the notion that bird song conveys meanings was first recognized by seers or shamans, whose influence among primitive peoples depended upon their professed ability to understand the language of animals."[11] Thus, bird speak is a rare gift among humans reserved for the very few, while the rest of humankind only hears the gibberish.

The song of birds is especially cherished by poets, probably because birds are the only creatures whose sound patterns are close enough to those made by humans, which convinces us that bird song is like human language in some way or another. The song of the poet has often been considered otherworldly in comparison to that of birds. In some respects, the poet shares the same language as the birds in that they are both divinely inspired. On a deeper level, bird song shares with music and poetry aesthetic qualities that are capable of arousing powerful feelings and spiritual awakenings. At the dawn of the Romantic Era, exalting intuition over reason, poets approached the shaman's ecstatic identification with birds as a revived method of discovering truth. The song of birds became, as it had once been for primitive peoples, a mysterious source of profound meaning and feeling.

In her fantastic book *Crows*, Candace Savage explains how crow vocalizations are "earthy," studded with what sound to us like consonants and vowels, as if their caws and "quorks" were pronouncements in some unintelligible

---

11. Leonard Lutwack, *Birds in Literature* (University Press of Florida, 1994), 46.

tongue.[12] The mysterious nature of bird speak is what captivates us as we strain to hear what on earth they're *really* talking about. It is precisely this mystery that keeps many people fixed upon birds' natural peculiarities, and may be, in some small way, what helps in their conservation today. As the world of science strains to hear what the birds have to say, the world as a whole grows more and more inclined to the possibility of one day understanding birds. All of these cultural parallels allow us to glimpse the archetypal imagery and meaning of the winged ones in generations of shamanic practices, making the bird one of the oldest symbols for spirit, magic, and divinity in human culture. No matter how the world around us changes, birds will continue to fascinate and delight us as spiritual beings bound to a flightless existence.

## The Bird Dance

While studying the cultural history of the flamingo, I came across a video of a group of flamingos dancing together. Needless to say, it was something impossible to forget. Although the large pink crowd was impressive, gliding across the watery plains in formation, what impacted me more was the bird's effortless ability to really enjoy the moment without a care of who might be watching.

Aside from the obvious visual power of bird dance, it also has a deep spiritual significance as a way of merging human energies with that of other forms of life. The movement of birds has inspired an enduring desire in the human

---

12. Candace Savage, *Crows* (2005) 15.

soul to imitate their marvelous twists and turns, and bird dances have been found all over the world as a profound appreciation for the beauty of bird life. "Dancing an animal" is one of the oldest ways to connect to the powers of nature, and is at the heart of shamanic practices everywhere. The cultural traditions of bird dancing are taken directly from bird dances seen in the wild, and much modern dance has taken its cue from this amazing natural phenomenon. The dancer attempts to capture the bird's essence or spirituality by imitating the hopping, flapping, and whirling of birds in nature as they dance for, or with, potential mates. Anyone with an understanding of wildlife knows that *many* creatures dance, but birds seem to take center stage as the earth's finest movers and shakers. The entire universe is governed by rhythm, responding instinctively to everything in nature. For the birds, dance is a process of connecting to other members of their species. It also stimulates courtship and gives the birds a chance to show off their skills, physical strength, boldness, and affection. They have mastered the rhythms of dance and hold their viewers enraptured by their grand displays. Some birds will grow more elaborate plumage just for the purpose of courtship, as a human will sport their finest clothes and jewelry.

The crane dance is possibly the oldest and most enduring bird dance imitated in human culture, with archaeological evidence suggesting early crane-dancers in the ancient town of Catal Huyuk (7500–5700 BCE). For the cranes, dancing is an all-encompassing experience, and cranes have been known to join in a dance when another begins—finding the whole process hopelessly addictive and joyful. They will fling objects in the air with their bills as they hop, flap, whirl, weave, and spread their large, magnificent wings. Crane dancers have performed these same moves in cultures as diverse as ancient China, Siberia, Africa, and Japan. In Greek legend, Theseus was said to have performed a crane dance in Delos after slaying the Minotaur, imitating the twistings and windings of the great bird with the young Athenians. In ancient Greece, the circular movements of the crane dance symbolized the changing seasons and the eternal passing of time. The arrival of cranes in the spring represented the sun god's resurgence, and people danced the *geranos*, or crane dance, to acknowledge the circle of life that encompasses both fertility and death.

The *blue jay* became a culture hero for several of the interior Salish tribes of Canada and parts of the United States who once honored this bird in an annual blue jay dance. Hop-dancing until overwhelmed by blue jay power, the shamans fled, twittering, and had to be captured and brought back to the medicine lodge. After they had regained their senses, they were able to perform cures and grant wishes for their people.

The T'boli people of South Cotabato on the island of Mindanao perform a bird dance during planting and harvesting that imitates the flights and hops of the tabaw bird. Another dance found here is the *Kadal Blelah,* in which the women dancers portray the *blelah,* a mythical bird that consolidates within itself the feather coloration of all known birds.

The Manchu shamans of China commonly invoke and make offerings to hawk and eagle deities. It has also been documented that the Manchu invoked the following bird deities: water birds, "wind" and "field" birds, and gold and silver-tongued birds. The following is from a description of a hawk dance performed by a Manchu shaman in China, a wonderful example of the intensity of the invocatory dance:

> The shaman puts on his magic costume … decorated with three birds, from which a dozen or more red or green colored ribbons hang … The shaman begins his invocatory dance. Carrying two drums … the shaman begins the invocation. The shaman beats the drums whilst dancing and shortly thereafter, the shaman achieves an altered state of consciousness. At this point the god of hawks is manifest … The shaman extends his arms outwards and flaps them. Occasionally, the shaman turns around with arms wide open, as the hawk god circles in the sky. By now the shaman has identified himself completely with the deity invoked and the hawk deity is completely present. The shaman as hawk god, steps up onto two tall tables, and still flapping his arms, prepares to fly.[13]

The Manchu shaman illustrates the power of the dance to become an embodiment of the bird spirit, which enables him to take into himself the bird's powers.

In Armenian tradition, there are descriptions of dances related to the worship of birds. The *bird ancestors* cult, and

---

13. *The Dances of Manchu Shamans* (Institute of Ethnic Literature, 2003–2009).

the idea of the Armenians' protection and ties of blood with them, feature prominently in their belief system. During the Middle Ages, there were two words for *dance: par* and *kavav,* the latter meaning *partridge.* An essential part of these bird dances was jumping, having originated from totemic dances in which the dancers disguised themselves as partridges. Cover pages from some manuscripts of the Middle Ages depict several images of dancers in bird masks, holding branches of a sacred tree in their hands. The dancing traditions of today have retained many steps that imitate the swaying gait of a bird. The pantomimic dance of Armenian *araghil,* meaning stork and usually performed by a man, is described as follows:

> The dance involved some disguise, the performer, squatting and taking a shepherd's crook, was then covered with a sheepskin coat turned inside out. The dancer put his hand and arm with the staff in one of the sleeves. The end of the staff that jutted out was wrapped in rags so that it looked like a stork's head. The dancer jumped to the music, swaying the staff. In this way he imitated the gait of a stork and the movements of its head. [14]

Another totemic bird dance, the *kryngaven,* imitates some of the behaviors of the crane, such as the relationship between a mother crane and her young.

The eagle dance of the Pueblos is thought to be a part of an ancient ceremony relating to rain and the growth of

---

14. *Performing Arts,* pg. 70

crops. Most of the Pueblo eagle dancers actually simulate eagles, wearing complete wings of eagle feathers, painting their bodies, wearing eagle down, and placing a beak atop their heads. Within the Lakota tribes, the eagle has long been honored in an eagle dance, performed by men wearing eagle feathers in their hair, and carrying fans made from eagle tail feathers. In the pheasant dance of the Cherokee, the dancers beat the ground with their feet in imitation of the drumming sound made by the bird. According to the Cherokee story, there was once a winter famine among the birds and the animals. They were near starvation when a Pheasant discovered a holly tree loaded with red berries (a favorite of the pheasant). The pheasant called his companion birds and they formed a circle about the tree, singing, dancing, and drumming with their feet in token of their joy. This is how the pheasant dance came into being. Many Indian tribes also honor both the dances of the prairie chicken and the grouse in the prairie chicken dance.

## Final Thoughts on Bird Shamanism

You can find books everywhere on how to become a shaman. You can spend thousands of dollars on workshops telling you how to become a shaman. In reality, you cannot become a shaman through a book or a workshop—end of story. You can, however, begin to understand how shamans communicate with animal spirits, and the profound effects animals of all kinds can have in your life by imitating ancient practices. By imitating these old practices, you will change your perception of the cosmos around you, and thus effect positive change within the whole. I am not a shaman, nor do I pretend to be one. I have, however, spent many years studying shamanic practices, animal totems, and the powers of animal spirits throughout the world. That does not make me a shaman, only an inspired outsider of a way of life that cannot survive in a technological society.

If you would like to become more closely connected to the ways of the shaman and the ways in which they harness the spiritual powers of birds, you must do your homework. There are no shortcuts, as popular media would suggest, to accomplishing an amazing spiritual awareness of the universe around you.

The most profound way to start a relationship with bird spirits, and the spirit of nature as a whole, is to *observe*. Really look closely at the way things in nature work. Observe the way a bird makes its nest by gathering an abundance of resources; watch the way a good rainfall will bring up to the surface a great feast for the robins; and admire the way the great birds of prey can soar effortlessly on the wind, or the way birds communicate with each other through songs, dances, and noises. So much goes unnoticed by the human eye and ear, which is why many birds and animals are taken for granted.

Once you have altered your perception of the wild through long observation, meditation, and study, you will begin to notice how birds of different feathers get your attention. You will see a hawk, or dozens of hawks, before any big life change. You will notice the brilliance of the hummingbird at those times in your life when happiness and joy has slipped from your awareness. The appearance of birds in your life as teachers will always coincide with your readiness to hear the message.

4

Birds in
Magic and
Religion

*Among the Romans not a bird,*
*Without a prophecy was heard.*
*Fortunes of an empire often hung*
*On the magician's Magpie's tongue,*
*And every crow was to the state*
*A sure interpreter of fate.*

—WINSTON CHURCHILL

Many of the superstitions we know today involving birds have been passed down for centuries, and many cultures actually still adhere to traditional beliefs regarding animals and their spiritual attributes today. Their fascinating history, and the cultural diversity of bird goddess mythology made exploring birds in the magical arts a treat for me. I wanted to know why birds were chosen time and time again to aid in the acquisition of magical powers, and how they have influenced modern day stories and beliefs.

The terms "magic" and "religion" often coexist in ancient cultures. It must be remembered that most prominent ancient cultures were pagan, and so magic will refer to the earth-based beliefs and practices of those cultures. Take ancient Rome, for example, as referred to in the above quote from Churchill. Rome's entire political and religious foundation was based on its pagan beliefs, handed down from civilizations like Greece.

Many of these beliefs centered around oracles, or prophecies, in which birds were the most integral part. Many people have told how birds can predict, and even control, the weather by bringing the rains and the thunder. To the peoples of the ancient world it would have made perfect sense that birds controlled the skies. They navigated the upper worlds with ease, seemingly disappearing into the upper world to converse with gods, goddesses, and other divine beings.

From the viewpoint of a pre-technological mind, the very act of flying would have been magic in the grand scheme of everyday human affairs. Winged creatures were sources of natural power and companions in magical works—able to bring the powers of the sky gods down to earth. Often, they were links to the gods themselves, and thus were privy to all of their secrets and wishes.

Birds were used for magical purposes in many different ways. The chapter on shamanism in this book gives you a good idea of the importance of bird paraphernalia (with beak, wings, and feathers) and how it endows the wearer with the bird's special powers, each part signifying a different spiritual quality.

In many cultures, bird parts were consumed in magical and healing rituals as well, and were symbolic of deities in physical form. Those who wished to take on the spirits of prophetic animals swallowed the most effective parts of them—the eyes, hearts, and flesh of birds were most sought after. It was believed that the hearts of eagles brought courage, the flesh of crows and owls imparted wisdom, and the flesh of hawks lent visual acuity to the consumer. The bones of birds were also considered magical aids, and many bird bones have been found that were carved into flutes producing a high-pitched sound. Some of these bones were engraved with the chevron, an ideogram associated with the goddess dating back into the Neolithic era. Music from these bird-bone flutes, enhanced by other piping instruments and accompanied by drums, are believed to have been used at sacred festivals celebrating the return of the water birds in spring.

The Cherokee Indians utilized the powers of birds for many practical as well as spiritual reasons, and birds were prominent figures in Cherokee magical formulas, songs, and incantations designed to influence the course of love, hunting, illness, and other human affairs. The Cherokee invoked the osprey, the kingfisher, and the eagle to ensure fishing success; the indigo bunting and the bluebird to control the wind; the hummingbird to shorten long journeys home; and their mythical raptorial bird, the Dhla:nuwa, along with the purple martin and great crested flycatcher for success in the ballgame. In Cherokee culture, the purple martin played a key role in the mythical ball game between the birds and the other animals.

## Birds in Egyptian Magic

Ancient Egypt has always been a pleasure to investigate, and anyone seeking a good history of birds in magic should continue to explore the topic beyond this book. It is among the most mysterious of religious traditions, and is filled with bird deities and magic. The falcon-headed god is easily recognizable to most people, and shows the very ancient reverence for this particular bird of prey.

The religion and magic of Egypt were crucial parts of their societal foundation, as they were in Greece and Rome. Images of the falcon and hawk were painted in tombs, palaces, and temples, and, like the sea-eagles at Orkney, the falcon and the hawk had a symbolic relationship with death and regeneration.

Many rituals performed by the Egyptians were recorded in the famous *Book of the Dead,* which is the common name given to the funerary texts known as *Spells of Coming Forth by Day.* These ancient texts contained hymns, spells, and incantations designed for the deceased in the afterlife. Being such an integral part in the religion of Egypt, birds appear everywhere in the transformation spells contained in the texts. The purpose of these spells was that the deceased might take on the form of a bird after the physical body died. This was a common motif throughout the entire ancient world.

The following spells are from the *Book of the Dead,* and are the words of the great god Osiris. From the *Chapter for a heart-amulet of Seheret-stone* this spell describes the great Benu-bird of Egyptian mythology: "I am the Benu-bird, the soul of Re, who guides the gods to the Duat when they go forth. The souls on earth will do what they desire, and the soul of Ani will go forth at his desire." The Benu bird was a prototype of the Greek Phoenix and was considered the physical manifestation of the Sun god Re. It took the form of a heron in Egyptian art, and was said to regenerate himself with the appearance of the sun each day. The word *benu* is thought to derive from an Egyptian verb meaning *to rise,* or *to shine,* revealing its ultimate nature as a solar entity. [15]

This next spell is excerpted from *The Papyrus of Ani,* chapter 77, and is called *To Assume the Form of a Hawk of Gold*: "I ascend from the balcony as a hawk of gold coming forth from its egg. I have flown, I have alighted as a hawk of gold of seven cubits on its back, its wings [are] like southern emerald. I have come forth from Evening Boat, and I have brought my heart from the mountain of the east. I have alighted in the Morning Boat, and I have brought those who are in their company bowing down. I ascend; I am brought together as a beautiful golden hawk, phoenix-headed." From *How to Assume the Form of a Heron,* (*The Papyrus of Ani,* chapter 84–85), we read: "I am the soul who has created the Celestial Ocean, making his place in the underworld. My nest is unseen, I have broken the egg. I am the lord of millions of years. I have made my nest in the limits of the sky." All of these poetic texts reveal the magical importance of birds to the ancient Egyptians. It is fascinating to see how centuries-old beliefs revolving around the powers of birds were used in everyday life. These texts reveal an enduring love for avian life and a deep respect for the gifts they bring from beyond the boundaries of our understanding.

## Birds in Mithraism

Mithraism is another one of the ancient mystery cults that moved throughout Rome from the first to the fourth centuries

---

15. Karl Richard Lespius, who first coined the term "The Book of the Dead" in 1842. Edward Naville, who published the first full standard edition in 1886.

AD. Originating in Persia, it was a great rival to Christianity in the last stages of the Roman Empire. The symbolic nature of Mithraism makes it an interesting addition to this book, similar to the stages of alchemy, which will be explored later in this chapter.

Like the initiation of the alchemists, the members of the Mithraic cult were taken through seven stages of ascending initiations, patterned upon ancient shamanic grades of met-empsychosis (or transmigration of the soul). The Brotherhood of Ravens later became the first of seven initiations in the religion, and was sometimes called the Corax, or Raven degree. This stage, like the first stage of alchemy, symbolizes the death of the initiate and his rebirth into the spiritual world. We will see later in the book just how prominent the crow and the raven became in subsequent religions as birds of death. The followers of the religion gave the same attributes to the raven (or crow) that the alchemical stages of transmutation had done in other traditions. The raven was believed to be an incarnation of Verethragna (the god of battles), and raven feathers became a popular talisman among initiates. The meditations of this stage required the initiates to mentally transform themselves into the raven and many would have worn a mask of the raven to better connect with its magical energies. Mithras shared the association with crows with the Graeco-Roman solar deity Apollo; in secret ceremonies, people dressed up as crows or ravens and would dance around an underground altar.

## Birds in the Bible

Early Christianity, taking many traditions from the old pagan Rome, adopted some similar beliefs about the powers of birds. Many were transformed into symbols of Christianity or as emblems of Christ, the Virgin Mary, or the Holy Spirit, making their earlier reverence within the old pagan mythologies devoid of meaning and power. Even with the Christianizing of bird symbolism, the impact of birds remained a large part of later religious iconography. The Virgin Mary, for example, as an archetypal mother image, is closely connected to the dove within the church. The Virgin Mary and the Greek goddess Aphrodite share common symbolism, particularly that of the dove, and like many other goddess images, the Virgin Mary is considered among scholars to be another descendant of the Paleolithic bird goddess. The symbol of the dove was used often in early Christian times in mosaics and catacombs. The dove's symbolism of peace originates from the Bible and the story of the ark, as it was the dove that returned with the olive leaf signifying the end of the flood: "And the dove came in to him in the evening; and, lo, in her mouth was an olive leaf plucked off; so Noah knew that the waters were abated from the earth." (Genesis 8.11)

Within Christianity, birds signify the presence of God—the dove being an emblem of the Holy Spirit at the baptism of Christ, and the sparrow, who represents God's love for even the smallest of creatures. The eagle was perceived as symbolizing the highest intellectual abilities of the human mind—that is, the ability to understand and have a clear perception of God.

In the story of the ark, the raven was the first bird to be sent forth by Noah: "At the end of forty days Noah opened the window of the ark which he had made, and sent forth a raven; and it went to and fro until the waters were dried up from the earth."[16]

The raven and the dove were used often in the Bible to represent those who are good and bad, or clean and unclean within the world. The stork was a symbol of the Annunciation and also came to represent Mary's virtuous qualities of piety and chastity. The goldfinch was a symbol of the passion of Christ because it eats thorns and thistles; Raphael's painting "Madonna of the Goldfinch" shows a baby Jesus stroking a goldfinch.

## Familiars

There are many ways we can harness the power of birds in our daily lives. Those involved in traditional magic will already know about the wonders of having a bird as a familiar—aiding in the creation and power of magical spell work and rituals. The familiar is one of the most prevalent images found within magical fields. It has been seen everywhere—from the ravens of Apollo and Odin to the little owl diligently perched on the shoulder of Athena. Birds have forever been the companions of gods, magicians, and shamans, helping them reach the heights of concentration, spiritual journeying, and contact with the other worlds.

The familiar is an animal who gains magical importance when summoned to service by a magician, sorcerer, god, or

16. Genesis 8: 6–7, New Oxford Annotated Bible, 1977

shaman for ritual work and spell casting. They provide a point of contact with the animal world, teach the magical worker animal ways, and act as parent figures to the shape shifter. The word familiar is derived from the Latin word *famulus*, which translates as *attendant*. In some traditions, the familiar makes itself known at the completion of an initiation, or as is common in more modern times, it will show itself when the magician requires its powers or wisdom in some area of life. Familiars are traditionally acquired in initiation or after the attainment of a certain level of magical skill. They are shape-shifted spirits that will only serve those to whom they are bonded.

In the earliest writings about witches, the creatures most strongly associated with witchcraft were connected to the underworld. The blending of magical consciousness between the witch and the familiar can open doorways to other realms and can accomplish works of magic in the material realm as well as the astral plane. Birds are often chosen as familiars due to their multidimensional flight; in the same way they are chosen by shamans for soul travel. Birds may carry healing energies from the shaman to a patient, or messages to and from the spirit realms. In ancient Greek mythology, the raven was the familiar of Apollo, the god of healing and prophecy. In southern Africa, the owl was usually considered the bird of sorcerers. In many other places, the owl is looked upon as being associated with witches and wizards.

# Augury

## *Bird Divination in Ancient Greece and Rome*

In the early centuries of Graeco-Roman civilization, bird divination relied less upon solidified interpretations and more on intuition. The dramatic appearance of a bird at a critical political or military moment would be regarded as a message of fate and divined accordingly by the *augur*. The augurs of ancient Greece and Rome were priests of the state who divined the will of the gods by observing the behavior of birds. They were extremely important parts of society, and were often held in high esteem by rulers and citizens alike.

In ancient Roman society, it was the task of the augur to ascertain Jupiter's will by means of auspices. No political and military decisions were made without the direction of the birds, and the augurs were consulted during times where important decisions had to be made. The political leaders of Rome needed reassurance that their actions would meet with favor among the gods, lest divine retribution be set against them and their empire. Augury became so important in ancient Rome that the official College of Augurs practically ran the affairs of state for many years. Scott Cunningham describes the traditional procedure for summoning a bird omen in ancient Rome:

> The bird diviner sat in a tent situated on a hill. Wearing a special robe, he described an area in the visible sky with an augural staff; within these bounds the omens were to occur. After pouring out libations of wine, a prayer was uttered beseeching the god

Jupiter to "grant that there be unerring signs within the boundaries that I have described." According to the appearance of birds and their behavior, the augur stated that "the birds approve" or "the birds disapprove."[17]

Roman augury concerned only birds. The first type of augury was observing the flight patterns of birds, mainly eagles and vultures. The second type involved the calls of birds, which was largely restricted to owls, crows, ravens, and chickens. In the time of Alexander the Great, crows or ravens were said to have led the fearless conqueror to the temple of Ammon in Egypt, and later foretold his death by fighting beside the walls of Babylon. Aside from the formal practice of birds in augury, they were believed to utter warnings and prophesies—a power derived from their contact with the omniscient gods and the souls of the dead.

## Augury in China

In China, during the Han Dynasty (104 BC), a post was established naming an officer *Perfect Grand Augur*. This officer was in charge of divination and other rituals that were used to influence state policy.

## Augury in Tibet and India

In Tibetan augury, the diviners interpret the calls made by crows. If the bird heralds some calamitous event or outcome, offerings are made to the crows in order to prevent the forewarned ill fate (the common offering consists of the flesh of

---

17. Cunningham, *Divination for Beginners* (Llewellyn, 2003).

a frog). The crow and raven are prominent in many older forms of divination due to their seeming ability to predict rain, or at least herald its coming. The ancients observed that the crow and raven would utter a peculiar sound just prior to a rainfall, and if a storm was imminent they would fly back and forth in restless motion. The crow and raven were also regarded as exceptional navigators. The connection of crow auguries with the cardinal points may have arisen from the very ancient observation of the crow's sense of locality, and its use in discovering land. Indian navigators even kept birds on board ship to dispatch them in search of land.

In Tibet, the raven is still called the protector of religion. The following is a translation of an Eastern text describing the role of the raven in Indian and Tibetan religion:

> The Raven is the protector of men, and the officiating priest ... of the order of the gods ... The venerable of the Gods conveys (his will) by means of the sound-language (of the Raven) ...
>
> The officiating priest is in possession of the knowledge of the gods ... and it is the bird who is his helpmate ... Truthful in his speech, he proves trustworthy, for the Raven is a bird of Heaven; He is possessed of six wings and six pinions ... His sense of sight is keen, and his hearing is sharp.
>
> ... he is able to teach (mankind) the directions of the gods. There is for man but one method of examining (the sounds of the Raven), and you may hence have faith and confidence (in his auguries)![18]

18. *Bird Divination in Tibet, Laufer*

In Southern India, the incessant cawing of a crow atop a house foretells the arrival of a guest, and the woman of the house will prepare more food in anticipation. The Rig-Veda ascribes the bird crying in the quarter of the fathers (the south) as being a summons of the fathers (ancestors) themselves.

## *Europe*

The ancient Celts were said to have a system of bird divination that resembled those found in ancient Rome. Cave paintings have been found in the Camonica Valley of northern Italy belonging to the Bronze and Iron Age Celts that portray ravens speaking to humans. Augury by ravens appears commonly in the British Isles, and the system is remarkably similar to that found in contemporary Tibet, where ravens are often watched for omens of luck or approaching visitors.

Now that you have some background on the role birds have played in Pagan religion and spirituality, we move into a detailed look at birds in alchemy— that most mystical and symbolic of magical endeavors.

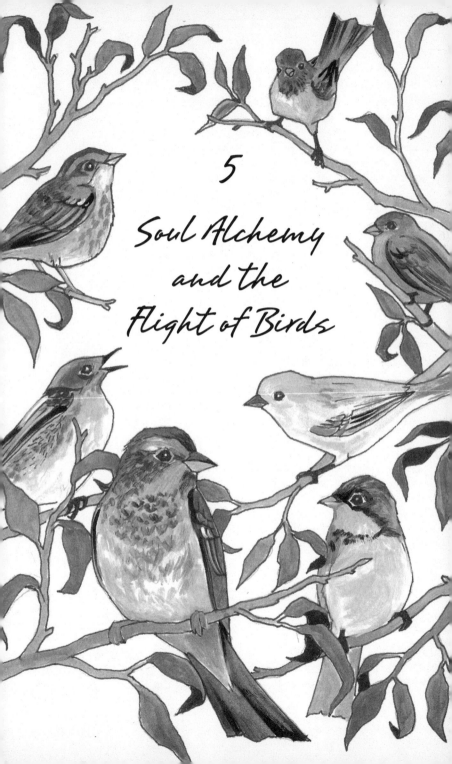

5

Soul Alchemy
and the
Flight of Birds

*I had discovered....that their doctrine was no mere chemical*
*fantasy, but a philosophy they applied to the world,*
*to the elements, and to man himself.*

—W. B. YEATS, *ROSA ALCHEMICA*

Because birds are such a prominent part of alchemy, I devoted a whole chapter to this old symbolism. For those unfamiliar with alchemy, it is technically the ancient scientific tradition in which base metals were turned into gold, or at least an attempt was made. The foundation of alchemy, as a science seeking to transmute the base into a higher form, became a metaphor for spiritual evolution and transformation. This "soul alchemy" resembles many spiritual traditions that emphasize the process of enlightenment, attainment, or becoming. Birds would naturally be the most appropriate representatives for such a fantastic goal.

The ancient alchemist saw in the flight of birds the nature of the human soul, transcending the realm of earth to attain new heights within the heavens. Their language was secret, using only symbolism to hide the deep spiritual truths of such transformations from the uninitiated masses. Soul alchemy is not something hidden from the world however, but speaks of the processes of inner transmutation that we all undergo on a continual basis, and the degrees of awareness that each process brings with it. The alchemists call it "The Great Work." As continually growing beings, these stages are inevitable. It is the hero quest and the breaking free from the bonds of physicality.

The birds that appear on the alchemical stage give much insight into the processes they represent. Their messages seem to parallel their spiritual significance outside of this mysterious tradition, revealing the eternal archetypal quality of birds. The most consistent of imagery is the crow, or raven, who invites us from the comfort of mortality into the eternal void where self-realization begins. The crow's appearance in alchemy is akin to those who encounter crow or raven as a spirit guide. These birds insist that a death occur—a death that need not be feared, but embraced as a new beginning. Those who accept the dying of the self have embraced the medicine of crow and raven. The other birds here include the peacock, the swan, the pelican, and the mythical phoenix.

A good way to understand the steps of alchemy, or soul transformation, is to walk through each of them as unique entities. The meditations that follow are designed to help you better understand the inner processes of soul alchemy. It may be a good idea to record them prior to the meditation and play them back to yourself during the exercise.

# Crow

### *The Nigredo Experience*

The black crow is symbolically the beginning of the Great Work of soul alchemy. This stage indicates the initiate's first encounter with her or his "inner space" through withdrawing from the outer world of the senses in meditation, and entering what is initially the dark inner world of the soul. *Nigredo*, or blackness in the alchemical sense means decomposition and putrefaction. By the penetration of the external fire, the inner fire is activated and the matter starts to putrefy. The body is reduced to its primal matter. This process may also be called "cooking." The black earth is closed up in a vessel, or flask, and then heated. It is often pictured as a process of death in the old alchemy texts, which makes the black crow the stepping out of physical awareness and the restrictions that bind us to the physical body.

## Meditation—Nigredo: Meeting the Crow

This meditation demonstrates the inner processes of *Nigredo*. It is where all things reside before they become manifest in three-dimensional reality. Here you will meet crow as your guide through the first stage of soul alchemy. This meditation is best performed at night with the absence of all sources of light. This will enable you to grasp the experience of darkness in its entirety.

> *Be still with your surroundings. Observe all of the "things" you grasp as tangible, real, permanent. Observe the walls, the floors, and the ceilings—your physical boundaries in earth-time. Now turn off all the lights. Close your eyes. Breathe. Allow your breath to be whatever it needs to be. Open your eyes. Observe the blackness that now surrounds you.*
>
> *Watch the tricks of the eye that move before your face. You will see patterns, colors, perhaps even visions.*

*Your mind is always seeking a "something" that places it in space and time. But these will slowly fade into darkness, for they are fleeting and transitory. Your mind begins to accept the nothingness before it. Look into the blackness—there is Crow. Crow surrounds you as you embrace the darkness. Welcome Crow into the space, but know that it is not your space. The walls, floors, and ceilings have gone, for you are now within the vastness of the eternal womb of creation, where all things are born, and to where all things must return at death. Embrace this darkness as the supreme emptiness of the universe. At this point, think of all the labels that you have appointed to yourself—the mental constructs of beauty, intelligence, strength, and talent that are slowly drifting outward from your ego. Hand them lovingly to Crow, who devours into himself that which has become the construct of the ego-mind. This will perhaps be the longest part of the meditation. Work with it until you can separate yourself from the images you have created with the physical mind. You are slowly becoming a part of the darkness where Crow resides. Now begin journeying with Crow through this space, and allow yourself to see all of the potential of this emptiness. Look closely as Crow shows you the thought patterns that form all things in the three-dimensional world. Stay in this place until you have understood the power of nothingness, of darkness, of the primordial abyss. Now, watch all of these things— these possibilities and desires slowly pass away. They are returning to that same blackness from which they came as mere things that have found no tangibility in your mind. Stay here as long as you can, for it is here that the rigid concept of physicality must fall away. This is where you will pass from the Blackening into the Whitening of the swan. Thank Crow for his guidance, and allow him to move on.*

*Turn on the lights. Take a few moments to re-adjust to your surroundings. Make notes if you wish, so that you may follow your progress throughout every stage of your transformation.*

## White Swan

### Albedo

The second stage we encounter in soul alchemy is symbolically represented by a white swan, often termed the *Whitening*. This is the stage where the initiate first catches a glimpse of inner enlightenment. It is the first encounter with illumination—the brilliant light that shines in even the darkest places within the human psyche. The swan is the blending of the physical world with that of spirit. As the alchemist moves inward, the illumination of swan unites the male and female. In alchemical imagery, this is seen as two streams of water pouring into one basin.

The swan is a bird that is rarely seen in flight, but rather swimming upon the water's surface. In terms of the soul, the swan gracefully moves upon the soul's surface. The swan, seemingly bathed in purity, is our lifeline to the etheric worlds. When we entered into the physical world, we entered upon a world of duality. The Whitening stage brings all things back into harmony, into oneness. Albedo is the rising sun at midnight; it is the light that pierces the darkest cloud of psychological turmoil. The swan symbolizes hermaphroditism, or the marriage of opposites.

## Meditation—The Whitening: Meeting the Swan

In this meditation, you will enter *Albedo*, or the *Whiteness* of the alchemical process. This may be done during daylight, preferably at sunrise or during early morning. Remember, you are moving into the realm of light and the reunion of opposites in this meditation, therefore sunrise—the light coming out of the darkness—will be very symbolic for this exercise.

> *Once again, be still with your surroundings. If possible, look toward where the sun is rising, or where the sun sits in the sky. Become aware of the luminescence of this light and the scope of its power over the earth. Now, imagine that all things of the physical world bend, and then dissolve to this light. The light begins to take a form, that of a magnificent white swan. The appearance of the swan signals a time of union. Things once perceived as opposite are at once merging into one whole being. Light pierces through from the darkness, just as darkness emerges from the light. They are one and the same, neither able to exist without the other. So it is within us, the physical and the spiritual, are one force, only operating from different vibrations of energy. Observe the white swan before you. The silky white feathers that seem divine and oth-*

*erworldly. The swan moves gracefully around you, taking your entire being within its wings. The light from the swan is warm, comforting, eternal. Then, the swan moves away, floating through the expanse before you. Observe the seemingly flawless nature of this bird, and accept that it was created in harmony with the crow. The swan being light, the crow darkness, but born out of the same void as all other things. You can see now the lightness that is within everything: you, the earth, humankind, animal-kind. It all belongs to the same darkness and the same light simultaneously. You have experienced Whiteness, Albedo, and can really see that light of awakening from within. Bid farewell to the spirit of swan. Open your eyes and re-adjust yourself to three-dimensional reality.*

## Peacock

### The Iridescence

The third stage of the soul's alchemical transmutation belongs to the peacock, who represents the awakening to the inner world of color. Having reached the light of swan out of the darkness of nigredo (crow), the alchemist becomes aware of the astral world of the ever-changing patterns of color, shifting and moving with the energy of creation. This is often considered the turning point in the alchemical process, as this is where the alchemist realizes the importance of the inner world as it shapes and transforms the outer world of three-dimensional reality.

## *Meditation—Iridescence: Meeting the Peacock*

This phase is symbolized by the peacock, its colorful and iridescent tail representing the blending of light and dark. All color comes from light reflecting upon dark, and is also seen in the beautiful plumage of raven and crow feathers, as well as hummingbird and magpie. Because this meditation involves your inner experience, time of day does not matter here. You have moved beyond the world of physicality and are awakening to the astral planes as experienced from within. This phase was sometimes falsely believed to be the attainment of enlightenment, but it is only the midpoint of the process and its somewhat illusory nature must not be confused with total illumination.

> *Close your eyes and enter the movement of your mind. Your thoughts run wildly, chaotic, seemingly with no purpose or direction. There appears also a myriad of colors, mixing themselves, separating themselves, evolving into images before your mind's eye. This rush of color comes from the merging of light and darkness, experienced in the earlier stages of Crow and Swan. Try not to attach yourself to anything you see, but allow a continual stream of visual impressions to flow through your mind. This may appear similar to the state of Nigredo, but the goal here is not dissolution, but rather the coming forth of the colors from within. Before you appears a great bird, taking its form from the chaos of color fusion. It is the peacock, signaling your progress in the Great Work by the release of the concept of duality. The Peacock reminds you that the*

*things of your mind are illusory. The colors are "tricks of the eye" just as the colors of its magnificent tail are only reflections of the sun—an optical illusion. Watch all of the colors, and the form of the Peacock blend together again as the illusory nature of mind collapses before you.*

*Open your eyes. Proceed to the Pelican stage that follows.*

## Pelican

### Working with soul forces

Stage four is perfectly represented by the pelican, as the alchemist must sacrifice himself to the inner being he is becoming. In this challenging phase, the image of the self must be changed and transformed, and essentially given up for the emerging spiritual Self that is forming.

### Meditation—Self-sacrifice: Meeting the Pelican

In this meditation you will encounter many things. This is where you go beyond the Self as you know it—as you created it—and allow the emerging spirit embryo to grow.

*Close your eyes. Allow your mind to drift once again from the material world around you. Pass through the astral world of Peacock, and step into the pure spirit that awaits.*

*Here you will meet the soul forces that are your essential being and your foundation.*

*Now, look at yourself in your mind's eye. Envision everything you believe yourself to be.*

*All the words you attach to your Self. All the things
you imagine you have, or are, or need. Now, envision
yourself throwing these things into a great, endless pool
of water.*

*This water absorbs the physicality of your cre-
ations. In front of you now, there is a large white bird
that approaches. It is a Pelican. She slowly skims the still
water, gently sending ripples across the surface. The Pelican then takes from the water all those things you cast
aside, and ingests them into her being. You have nourished this great bird of the waters and she is grateful for
the gifts. She extends her large bill toward you, and opens
it wide. She offers you a tiny embryo that glistens like the
brightest star in the universe.*

*The embryo is your soul in its purest state. It is
what you truly are when illusion collapses and the real
Self emerges. Thank the Pelican for her teachings as
you take the image of the embryo back into the world.
Open your eyes. Look into a mirror for a few moments
and notice how your perception of yourself has radi-
cally changed. You are ready for the final stage of soul
transmutation.*

## The Phoenix

### Perfection of the Great Work

This is the final stage of the alchemist's inner development.
The goal of the spiritual pilgrimage is the phoenix, the
feathers of which constitute a cure for anger and grief, a sort
of universal medicine which constitutes bitterness and suffering in the beginning, but at its end awaits a heavenly joy.

This mythical bird represents immortality and rebirth, and was adopted by the alchemists as a symbol of the final stage of the Great Work, whose end resulted in complete illumination and spiritual awareness. In mythology, the phoenix was said to have arisen from its own ashes after burning in the flames of the funeral pyre. This is a classic symbol of rebirth around the world, and of coming forth renewed after death.

## Meditation—Meeting the Phoenix

*Close your eyes. Imagine yourself coming forth from the tiny embryo given to you by the pelican. You have allowed your true being to emerge anew, as a spiritual being cloaked in light. You can now see the forces of your soul beaming forth from your physical body.*

*You are spirit made flesh. The Self has dissolved into the world of pure Spirit. Before you flies a large bird, almost unreal to your eyes. It is the Phoenix, legendary for its powers of renewal, and only seen during the achievement of the Great Work.*

*The great bird flies over you, and drops a feather in your hand. The feather symbolizes the lightness of your new being. It is the true nature of the human soul, unbound to the physical world. You are no longer dependent upon your physical body as the foundation for your being, but you are a being of spirit within that body. Thank the Phoenix for signaling your alchemical goal, and return to the awareness of the world around you.*

6

Feathers

*Hope is the thing with feathers that perches in the soul, and*
*sings the tune without the words, and never stops at all.*

—EMILY DICKINSON, *HOPE IS THE THING WITH FEATHERS*

As a self-proclaimed bird fanatic, finding feathers is like finding buried treasure. I must know instantly who it came from, and find a spot in my collection right away to display and preserve the priceless token of nature. Children, too, seem to gravitate toward feathers, and I will often share my gifts with my daughter and her friends. For such complex structures, feathers are unique and magnificent things to behold, and they provide a wide range of functions in order to ensure the survival of each bird species. From insulation and flight, to landing and diving, feathers are an all-purpose tool for birds.

Scientifically, feathers are epidermal growths that form the plumage of birds. They form in the tiny follicles of the outer layer of skin that produces keratin protein, and are perfectly designed by nature to insulate the body, promote flight and landing, camouflage, and attract potential mates through their often stunning visual nature. They are thought to have evolved from the scales of reptiles, and are the outstanding features that set birds apart in a world of their own. Spiritually, however, feathers have been given a complex array of meanings, and connect us earth-bound beings to the magical realm of air.

From a cultural standpoint, feathers are often used as symbols of spirit, freedom, divinity, magic, authority, and even as status symbols. The airy ineffability of the feather is a powerful symbol of truth and its vulnerability, and of the soul's weightlessness. Among many Native and aboriginal tribes, feathers clearly mark the identity of a tribe or band. The native peoples of New Zealand, Papua New Guinea, North America, and Africa still use feathers for ceremonial rites and initiations. In South America, feathers are worn at initiations and funeral rites, and are used by shamans as a source of power, to mark social identity, or to exercise political influence. In the Mayan tradition, three feathers adorned the crown of Mu, and the headpiece of Ra Mu, the King High Priest of Mu-Niven's Mexican stone tablet.

Wearing feathers is a reminder of the connection be-tween human and animal life. When the human body is clothed in feathers, one's thoughts turn toward the possibil-ity of release from this world. This is why many ancient sky deities were depicted with feather cloaks and bird compan-ions—they were symbolic of something beyond this world, and promised something bigger than what the human mind is capable of perceiving.

Feathers are light and of the air element, symbolizing the boundless nature of the soul. As complex as feathers ap-pear from a scientific viewpoint, they are enduring images of simplicity, lightness, and effortlessness. The single feather often worn by American Indians kept each warrior in touch with the world of spirit. They have been called "symbols of the accomplishment of rising from the terrestrial world, of being free of the gravity of the mundane world."[19] The wisdom of birds is symbolized by, and transmitted through, their feathers. Many healers and magical practitioners use them for a number of reasons, and although they carry much of the same spiritual properties, the bird from which the feather came must be understood and acknowledged before its proper use in spiritual affairs. Traditional shamans from all over the world use feathers regularly to aid them in removing disease from a patient's body, and to speed up the healing process. The traditional ceremony known as *smudging* (discussed below) is no doubt familiar to many people. by now, and is one of the most effective ways to clear energy.

Among the Pueblo Indians, prayer sticks, or prayer feathers, are made of willow, painted, and then feathers are attached with cotton. The *to'ai* consists of a stick of cane, with two turkey feathers attached.

During shamanic healing ceremonies, the shaman places four eagle or hawk feathers in the ground at each of the cardinal points around the patient's body. The shaman then sings and picks up each feather, one at a time, and touches it to the seat of pain on the patient. Some shamans will doctor sick persons with their eagle feather fans, where the healing power is transmitted through the healer's arms into the feathers, and then into the person's body.

Feather fans are often representative of particular deities, and are sometimes made by initiates for use by other initiates in a spiritual tradition. In African culture, feather fans represent the goddesses Oshun and Yemenja. The

---

19. Ted Andrews, *Animal Speak* (St. Paul, Llewellyn, 1993) 91.

peacock feather fan of Oshun, and the duck feather fan of Yemenja are used in order to cleanse in the name of those deities. These goddesses have the ability to remove obstacles through the ceremonial use of the sacred feather fans.

In the Maori culture of New Zealand, feather cloaks (*kahu huruhuru*) were symbols of Oceanic kings and were worn by the aristocracy. The most prized feathers for these cloaks were from the kiwi, particularly the rare albino. The Aztec and Mayan people often used hummingbird feathers, or their ashes, as expediters in magical work because of the rapid motion of the bird in flight. They would also use feathers to apply magical paints used in initiations. The color of the feathers worn by Mayans denoted the rank of the wearer; yellow feathers defined royalty; blue, the priesthood; and red feathers were worn by soldiers and nobles. In ancient times, yellow appears to have been the color of royalty in many parts of the world. Peacock feathers were worn as a symbol of official rank during the Ming Dynasty in China, and are commonly thought to represent the evil eye in many parts of the world.

## Feather Color Meanings

If you plan to incorporate feathers into any kind of spiritual work, the following color correspondence list will be of much service. As with any spiritual work, of course, your intuition will be your best guide.

*White feathers:* represent moon energy, purification, peace, and protection from spirit. Many shamans wear white as symbolic of their connection to the higher realms. In

South America, white seems to be primarily a shamanic color

*Red feathers:* stimulate the life force and represent vitality, action, energy, and power. In South America, red feathers may represent goodness, power, fertility, the blood of battle, sacrifice, and sexuality.

*Blue feathers:* are thought to stimulate psychic awareness and mental acuity. They bring about the energies of joy, peace, and calm, and are symbolic of water and the sky. In South America, blue feathers may symbolize the sky, water, ritual incense, and communication.

*Black feathers:* dispel negativity and will sometimes represent spiritual wisdom. Because many black feathers, like those of crow and raven, contain many other colors when seen in the light, they are symbolic of the void where everything is created, and have very mystical properties. In South America, black feathers can be associated with high rank and power, but may also represent negativity.

*Yellow feathers:* are symbolic of the sun's pro-creative powers, and also of joy, mental alertness, and prosperity. In South America, yellow feathers can evoke the sun, energy, and fertility

*Green feathers:* represent money, health, fertility, growth, and new life. In South America, green feathers are symbolic of vegetation.

*Brown feathers:* are typically used for connecting the element of air to the ground, and bringing the wisdom of spirit down to earth.

*Pink feathers:* are believed to attract the energies of love and open the heart's receptivity to loving experiences.

*Gray feathers:* represent neutrality as well as peace. They are considered a blending of earth (black) and spirit (white), and will aid in the joining of these forces for healing purposes.

## Types of Feathers

### Flight Feathers

The feathers of the wings and the tail are the most important feathers used in flight. These feathers are most often used in healing ceremonies because of the strength and power in controlling the air element. They are used for channeling energy into the area of the body that requires healing. Use flight feathers when strong energies are needed to clear negativity in the body or in a room.

### Tail Feathers

Tail feathers allow birds the ability to come back down to the ground. They offer birds the means of keeping their connection to the Earth Mother after soaring through the heights of father sky. As healing tools, tail feathers help us stay grounded upon the earth for daily living as we ascend in the ways of spirit. Working with bird medicine can create a sense of being out of touch, so grounding is essential in avoiding too many flights of fancy. Use tail feathers for concentration and for bringing yourself back down to the earth.

## A Word of Caution

Feathers used for healing purposes should *never* be obtained illegally or with harm done to the bird itself. Feathers will be gifted to you at the appropriate times in your spiritual progress, so be patient.

# Healing Ceremonies

Below is a list of bird feathers that are the most often used in healing ceremonies.

## Eagle Feather

Eagle feathers embody the energies of freedom and connection to the Great Spirit. Traditionally a symbol of the sun—a male entity—use eagle feathers for deep healing or strong energy blocks concerning imbalances of male energy. Eagle's connection to the sky and wind will aid in the removal of stagnant energy. I often use eagle feathers when the male principle is needed, or when physical action is required to get things moving from the plane of thought into the plane of tangible reality.

## Hawk Feather

Hawk is strongly connected to the goddess in the tradition of Wicca, and carries strong feminine energy. You may use hawk feathers to strengthen your connection with Mother Earth, and to heal blockages caused by an imbalance in female energies. Hawk feathers may also be worn in ritual for keen insight and intuitive abilities, and are wonderful tools to aid in focus and concentration. Combined with owl feathers, those of the hawk will enhance your dream life.

## Owl Feather

Owl feathers, from another bird associated with the goddess, are used in Wiccan rituals, especially those related to the moon or lunar cycles. Owl feathers will enhance any magical workings, particularly those that involve divination of any kind. Owl's feathers also hold strong energies of the night and death. Use them for release ceremonies, or hang them above your bed for dream work.

## Vulture/Condor Feather

Vulture is known as the purifier, so its feathers are used for ridding the body of impurities. Vulture feathers carry heavy medicine, and will work very strongly on the body, mind, and spirit that needs cleansing. This bird's obvious connection to death makes their feathers powerful tools that should be used with caution and respect.

## Swan Feather

Swan feathers are considered conduits of creative energy, inspiring poetic and musical ideals. Use swan feathers for artistic expression, or to heal wounds relating to self-esteem. Swan feathers will aid in enhancing clairvoyant abilities if worn or hung above the bed. With a strong connection to water, they are also excellent tools for resolving emotional stagnation.

## Hummingbird Feather

Often used to speed the healing process, these feathers rid the Self of disease, heaviness of spirit, and help bring a sense of joy back into the aura. Hummingbird feathers have always been used as love charms, and may help draw in the energies of love into one's life. They are excellent tools for opening the heart chakra, but must be used delicately, as hummingbird's medicine is very fragile. Use hummingbirds feathers with only the purest of intentions.

### Goose Feather

Goose is strongly connected to mythology and folklore. Its feathers aid the writer in the process of creation—use a goose quill pen to overcome writing blocks. As a water bird, goose holds many healing medicines regarding our emotional natures. Use goose feathers to release emotional baggage and unwanted negative feelings. Being migratory birds, their feathers may help in the processes of spiritual journeying.

### Ostrich Feather

The ostrich feather has an ancient symbolic meaning, and was the feather used by Ma'at to weigh the souls of the dead. Legend says that it was the lightness of the ostrich feather that made it an emblem of truth. Ostrich feathers are wonderful balancing tools. Being a flightless bird, its feathers help in finding practical ways to use spiritual knowledge, and connect the powers of air with the powers of earth.

### Peacock Feather

Peacock feathers are often used as meditation tools for the purpose of past life recall. The eye pattern on the tail feathers is said to represent psychic vision that can penetrate the boundaries of time and space.

7

Bird

Medicine

The term *bird medicine* may be a new concept for many of you, but it is a generalized term referring to the culturally recognized spiritual attributes of birds. Sometimes these attributes are called gifts or knowledge, guidance or wisdom, but always carry connotations of a higher set of qualities than just the usual biological structure.

As teachers, birds show us the power of faith in our lives. I spend hours watching birds, especially during the spring and summer months when all of nature seems to explode with activity. Birds are courting, mating, nesting, and playing, and provide countless opportunities to see nature work firsthand. Among my favorites to watch are the crows, magpies, waxwings, and finches because of their hilarious social antics and easy visibility, and the birds of prey, soaring above the mundane world on the hidden breath of the universe.

What a great lesson for the human mind—always fearful of the future.

The information about each bird in this chapter is a dynamic blend of culturally significant meanings. Much of what you will read gives specific reference to the culture or social group from which it came, but some is more generalized—an idea held by many different people around the world. I hope you will take this knowledge as a starting point in your own journey with the bird world. Their significance to you, however, will be more intuitive than factual, and essentially always open to interpretation.

The spiritual wisdom of birds is generally believed to involve the lessons of spiritual flight, personal freedom, and seeing life from a higher perspective. Every bird has its own unique lessons that need to be thoroughly understood before starting a spiritual or magical relationship with them. When beginning your work with birds on a spiritual level, it is important to remember not to rush your experience. Bird totems will choose those who can benefit from their teachings, and only when that person is ready for the medicine involved. Having a bird as a totem can be a very different experience from working with land animals. I hope you have already had some great experiences in that area. If animal medicine is a new concept for you, take the time to understand its powerful, primitive, and very ancient workings.

I have combined,in the following descriptions, the spiritual beliefs of each bird from the cultures that have celebrated them throughout history (and prehistory). Not every single bird will be listed, but the most prevalent birds in mythology, literature, and spirituality have been given due attention. I hope you will use this book as a springboard from which to start your own research and relationships with the avian world. The detailed descriptions that follow are designed to help you develop a deeper understanding of birds, as well as their ancient mythological and historical importance. It is also helpful to study the particular behavior, diet, and habitat of each bird to greater connect with your bird ally, as they are all very crucial to their wisdom and teachings.

The Birds
of Prey

The birds in this group have a significant position in our mythological history. Eagles, hawks, falcons, and owls have been deified, adored, imitated, and feared in every part of the world—as you will see in their detailed descriptions below. As predators, they carry a unique presence for those who study them closely, and have been highly respected and sought after as shamanic companions for thousands of years. They keep our attention lofty and unmoving, and inspire a sense of attainable heights in our earthly endeavors.

These birds can be very challenging and rewarding spiritual teachers. In a broad sense, they carry the teachings of expansiveness, power, fearlessness, ascension, and often solitude. I personally find great delight in working with these birds, and I find their natures very close to my own.

Birds of prey carry the lessons of death and the natural cycles of life. In Neolithic religion, the birds of prey played a very important role in the death process. People did not bury the dead immediately, but exposed their bodies on outdoor platforms. There, birds of prey would remove all of the flesh from the body, which was considered a necessary step in completing the natural cycle. These birds were respected as aiding the passing over of the dead so the next cycle of the soul's journey could begin.

When a bird of prey shows up as a guide, you will be asked to view your life from much higher ground. There are possibilities that you are not seeing from your current vantage point, and the high flight of one of these birds will be necessary to perceive the overall picture. Carefully study the unique attributes of each bird as you move forward in your connection with their powers, and consider the possibility of going beyond your preconceived notions of yourself in this process. Many people working with the birds of prey develop personal changes in many ways—even dietary adjustments are a possibility. These changes are normal for spiritual work with any predator totem, and are a sign of closer involvement with its energies and natural instinct; it is a crucial part of their wisdom and should be honored as such.

## Eagle

*medicine:* freedom, ascension, heightened perception

*family:* Accipitridae

*diet:* fish, carrion, rabbits, raccoons, beavers, ducks, geese, and other animals

*habitat:* seacoasts, rivers, lakes, and oceans

I personally am not visited by the eagle as often as I would like, but when this spectacular bird does show up, it is impossible to ignore the imminent lessons approaching. Eagle likes to appear to me in the dream time, leaving me feathers for my wandering soul to find and interpret. In one of my dreams, I had to climb to the top of a massive mountain, only to find the eagle soaring over its nest in complete power and solitude. Like this great bird, I relish the quiet spaces away from rest of the world. It is a herald of profound transformations in perception and the evolution of the soul.

As one of the largest birds to grace the earth, the eagle is often thought to be the most majestic of all winged creatures.

I once had the awesome experience of watching a bald eagle swoop down into the snow, trying to catch a panic-stricken gopher. I might have seen the outcome if I hadn't been driving, but the small glimpse of eagle in the wild was a fantastic show. In many spiritual traditions, the eagle is the personification of ascension, and will often come into the lives of those who are coping with new spiritual challenges or are required to attain new heights in some way.

With a wingspan of over two meters, eagle flies close to the sun, and was once believed to look directly into its powerful rays with perfect and unflinching focus. Eagle uses its powerful wings to soar up high on air thermals, allowing conservation of the energy needed for gathering food. Eagle medicine contains the lesson of reaching high without exhausting ourselves on the way up. Success is easily attainable, as demonstrated in the lofty, seemingly effortless flight of the eagle.

When searching for food, the eagle has been known to attack other birds and animals in order to take what they have for themselves. Those aligned to the eagle's path will go through many lessons involving selflessness in order to tame the heightened ego that comes from such a strong medicine. Eagle is also the companion of visionaries, but reveals the hidden risks of rising above the crowd. It is aloof and idealistic, preferring to nest much higher than everyone else. The need for a heightened perspective governs this bird's behavior, and it often steers clear of human disturbances at all costs. Eagle relishes the quiet places where it can observe the world in peace.

Eagles express a sort of hidden hierarchy that they rule diligently in the wild. Those with its energies, likewise, have an innate need to distance themselves from those they feel will not benefit their growth, which may make them seem egotistical to many on the outside of the nest. This hierarchy may come from eagle's reputation as a solar bird, and its ancient connections to solar deities around the world. In Celtic tradition, the eagle is associated with the sun god Lugh, whose name means "the bright one." The plumage of the golden eagle symbolizes perfectly these solar connections, while the coloring of the bald eagle grounds spirit to the earth.

Eagle has often been used as a national symbol or emblem due to its historical significance as a powerful bird of the heavens. It is recognized as a symbol for freedom, victory, and unrivaled power. To the Welsh, the eagle possessed great shape-shifting abilities, and due to the eagle's abilities to fly the highest and see the farthest, it has long been one of the most sought-after shamanic allies in the world. The Buryat people of Siberia revere the eagle as the first shaman sent by the gods to assist the healing of human beings. In the ancient Greek pantheon, the eagle represented the ruler of the heavens, Zeus, who is equated with Jupiter in Roman mythology. It is not surprising to see this bird an emblem of the ancient Roman legions, marching alongside many great leaders into battle. They were representative of military strength and victory over adversaries.

Native American mythology and symbolism is one in which we often see the strongest presence of the eagle. In many American Indian tribes, eagle was chosen by the

Creator to be the leader and the master of the sky. To receive an eagle feather is considered the highest honor, and eagle holds a special connection with Great Spirit. If you are blessed with an eagle feather, you have probably learned a great lesson, or survived an important challenge. It is also believed that wearing or holding an eagle feather shows respect for the Creator of all things, no matter what your idea of the Creator may be.

In the tradition of Earth Medicine, the eagle represents a powerful, spiritual energy. Because this bird soars so close to the sky, it is believed that it hears the voice of the Great Spirit and relays messages to the human world. Eagle medicine is about ascension and connection to the higher realms. Although all bird medicine and wisdom can be challenging, Eagle forces us out of the ordinary parameters of our existence and asks that we reach the sun—our inherent illumination—and awakening of spirit.

As a symbol, the eagle is used often as a comparison to something great, regal, and powerful. William Shakespeare, in *Richard II*, compares the mighty eagle to the king in the following passage:

> Yet looks he like a king: behold, his eye, as bright as
> is the eagle's, lightens forth controlling majesty.[20]

The eagle, being identified as the king of birds, has often been called the only companion for the kings of men. The eagle's sky-aspiring flight, towering place, and majestic ap-

---

20. Chambers, 1882, original from Princeton University, Editor John Miller Dow Meiklejohn.

pearance owe much to this regal reputation. Eagle medicine itself is a lofty ambition, and many people who are connected strongly with eagle wisdom fall many times before finally reaching the height of their ideals.

When studying the flight of the eagle, you will see that he does not soar straight to the top, but circles slowly upward, faithful that the currents of spirit will not falter. When the spirit of eagle calls to you, I suggest you keep your ego in check; pride will not carry you to the lofty places of the eagle. You must release your need to be in control, or to direct your evolution, so that you can truly ascend to the heavens like this magnificent bird of prey.

Eagle medicine may also point to a time of increased perception of other worlds and different states of consciousness. During the few times I encountered the eagle as a teacher, my dreams became extremely vivid, and somehow seemed to merge with my waking reality. Study the history of shamanic trances and rituals when working with the eagle to fully understand the ways in which we can bridge these boundaries of perception. You will experience with eagle a higher awareness than that of the ordinary physical mind. When I dream of the eagle, it is usually soaring in some silent lofty place, high above the human world, seemingly aware of multitudes of realities besides our own. These symbols and scenes illuminate the eagle's teachings of rising above normal perceptions of both ourselves and the universe around us.

Keep in mind the often solitary nature of this bird. You may be asked to step away from the crowd during your work with eagle and surrender to your inner resources and connection to the world of spirit. All of our great transformations as spiritual beings occur in the stillness of solitude.

Eagle's heightened awareness of the will of the universe teaches us the power of creation. You must be willing to use your intentions honestly to create that which is in your best interests, even if they at first appear to be too lofty or out of reach. Eagle teaches you to acknowledge your own power and ability to manifest what you desire, but ensuring your creations are in harmony with spirit and not the intent of the ego-mind. This *higher intent* is a challenging, yet inherent lesson of eagle and will not be easy to learn. You will be asked to operate from a place of high integrity and honest intentions in all that you do, say, or think. This is why the ego must surrender in the presence of eagle, or it will not take you far in its teachings.

Those who carry this medicine often have lofty ideals and will strive to live life from high places of success. Again, we find the challenges of ego, and the need to ascend in *spirit* and not through self-satisfying desires. When in balance with the universe, our ambition can lead us to great achievements that will benefit others as well as ourselves. Eagle reminds us that there are no real limitations in the world—we are spiritual beings and are free to create with ease and freedom. American Poet Langston Hughes once commented, "Hold fast to your dreams, for without them life is a broken winged bird that cannot fly." This is the heart of eagle medicine—reaching the place where we realize our own freedom to soar.

### Connecting with Eagle Medicine

Eagle is a powerful bird spirit, and learning to connect with its energies requires great patience and effort. Meditations will be of great help as you work with eagle, as this bird teaches the expansiveness of the mind and the ability to achieve altered states of perception. Imagine yourself from the viewpoint of eagle during your meditative work, soaring over the earth with great power and ease. Imagine the wind, a constant companion of the eagle, supporting the powerful wings of this bird and allowing him ascension to ever greater heights. As you move through eagle medicine, the power of spirit will likewise be *your* companion. Be receptive to the universe and the all-encompassing spirit of eagle in your life so that you may achieve the effortless flight of the king of birds.

## Owl

*medicine:* prophecy, magic, silence

*family:* Strigidae

*diet:* carnivorous—bats, birds, reptiles, rabbits, and other small animals

*habitat:* forested areas

(Snowy Owl habitat: open fields, marshes of the Arctic Tundra)

Owl will always be the dearest bird species to me, and I have had many sad and spiritual encounters with this magnificent bird of prey. The biggest impact came after a difficult rescue of a great horned owl on the side of an Alberta highway. I thought the bird was dead, so I pulled over for a closer look. As I approached, the owl lifted her head slowly, looked me in the eyes, and rolled over backwards as she began to lose consciousness. I managed to cover her with my sweater and gently get her into a box I had in my car. The owl suffered slowly as we awaited the wildlife rehabilitation drivers to arrive, and it was just as painful for me to see such a beautiful, wild creature lay so helpless in front of me. After the diagnosis, I learned of the massive head trauma she had suffered from her collision with a vehicle. Unfortunately, I never found out if she survived for release back into the wild, but her impact on me was heartfelt and enduring. I have picked up many great horned owls from the highways in Alberta, and all but that one never made it past the impact of the cars they hit. It is a sad fate, and one that increases every year around the world.

The owl has traditionally been very close to the spirit worlds, and associations between the owl, death, and magic are quite prominent and widespread. The barn owl in particular appears the most ghostly against the night sky with its eerie dark eyes, pale face, and white body. Historically, however, owls have not fared well at the hands of humankind. They have been feared because of their ancient connections with witches and magic, and even today owls cannot shake the many shadowy qualities that have been thrust upon them.

The vision of the owl is supreme, having the physical adaptations that allow them mastery of the realm of night. The owl possesses a large cornea and pupil which allows efficient collecting and processing of light. The retina of this bird's eye has an abundance of light-sensitive cells, and they are also equipped with three eyelids, giving them maximum protection. Their vocals are also astounding, and they produce a wide array of hoots, whistles, screeches, purrs, screams, snorts, and hisses. Being born night hunters, owls have a highly developed auditory system that allows them to discover the precise location of their prey. This *directional* hearing permits an extremely accurate detection of sounds, and allows for precision in hunting. Those who work with owl spiritually are usually able to detect subtle noises around them, being sensitive to sound frequencies. This clairaudience manifests in some way within the owl totem person, for eample as continuous buzzing sounds in the ears.

Because they are believed to have supernatural powers, the body parts of owls have often been used in folk medicines and magic rituals, and their ability to see in the dark became a metaphor for the oracular and divinatory powers of the Witch. Interestingly, the Greek word for witch, *strix*, is used to name one genus of owls, and its Latin derivative, *striga*, names the order *Strigiformes*, to which all owls belong. Due to the sacred nature of this bird in connection to the goddess, particularly in her crone-aspect, one of its many Gaelic names is *Cailleach oidhche* (crone of the night). The barn owl is *Cailleach-oidhche gheal*, "white old woman of the night." The sacred nature of the owl was eventually denigrated by the church in order to convert people from old pagan beliefs.

The owl is a very territorial bird, and will viciously defend its nest against any invader. This is why the ancient Romans looked upon the owl as a symbol for victory and success in battle. It was, of course, the enduring symbol of Athens, one of the most powerful cities in the ancient Greek world. Remains of mummified barn owls have been found in ancient Egyptian tombs, indicating their reverence for these birds as spiritual beings, or messengers from the afterlife. In Hinduism, the owl remains a symbol for cosmic spirituality, and the Cree Indians believed that the sounds of the boreal owl were a summons to the spirit world. The Incas, that fantastic ancient culture of Peru, venerated the owl for its beautiful eyes. Among the Oglala Sioux Indians, when a warrior excelled in combat he was allowed to wear a cap of owl feathers to represent his bravery.

A night bird, owl frequents the dark evening—the realm of things unknown. It is akin to the moon, being the light that shines forth in the darkness, and thus governs the realm of moon magic. These attributes, along with its mysterious night cry and mesmerizing stare, have earned it an evil reputation. As night hunters, owls gather strength from the twilight hours between dusk and dawn. Traditionally, these are the times when the spirit world is most accessible, which is why many rituals and spell castings are performed after dark. Owls can penetrate the darkness like no other bird, making them powerful allies. If you are aligned with this bird's wisdom, you will have an innate understanding of the human mind. Many owl people can penetrate the subconscious minds of others, revealing their true intentions, emotions, and thoughts. Owl people can see into the "dark" places of the human psyche as the owl sees its prey moving in the dark of night.

If owl chooses you as a student, you are to become aware of all that moves in the dark. These could be hidden motives, thoughts, or emotions within you or others that have been kept from the light of awareness. Or, there may be a hidden gift of clairvoyance and magic that needs nurturing when owl appears. Owl is the guardian spirit of many magicians and shamans, and often portends a time of deep learning or training in the ways of magical sight and manifestation. Owl people can pierce the normal boundaries of space and time, and are quite adept at traveling back and forth between worlds.

Having the owl as a totem is not always an easy experience. In fact, I consider owl's medicine to be among the most challenging. In the wild, owls are often harassed and physically attacked by smaller birds due to their predatory and nocturnal natures. They are seen as constant threats, and live, essentially, on the outside of the everyday world. Owl people are usually solitary and must sometimes take hits from those without a firm spiritual understanding. Most of the predatory bird totem people experience these challenges, as they are powerful and threatening to many others who have chosen not to pursue the expansiveness of spiritual realities.

Owl spirit guides will often visit their human companions in the dream time. This is where the owl imparts wisdom through dream symbolism and imagery. The owl person must learn about archetypes—universal symbolic images—in order to decipher owl's hidden messages. Symbolism is also at the crux of magic, and should be studied carefully by the owl person.

Owl people are often troubled by an innate wisdom of the universe that finds no expression or validation in the affairs of humans. They disdain many social structures, and find it difficult to maintain close relationships with people in general. Many people aligned with owl find that retreat from the disenchanted world is the greatest path to understanding, and owl will often guide those with its medicine away from their normal preoccupation with everyday activities by instilling a sense of disappointment in the owl soul person. This sense of discontent eventually leads the owl person into a deep exploration of the hidden worlds. The spirit of owl seems to haunt their very souls, as if a constant reminder of the illusory nature of life on earth.

## Snowy Owl

Although this bird carries much of the same medicine as the entire owl species, there are some gifts unique to the snowy owl. As a diurnal hunter, the snowy owl inhabits the realm of day, making its cycle of power different than most other owl species.

The snowy owl, with its home in the Northern circumpolar region, has special connections with the direction north, and is a crucial part of the food web of the tundra ecosystem. In the Celtic tradition, north is the place of tempering, challenge, testing, refinement, and discipline. It is the place of battle, where we shed our fears, address our addictions, and move from emotional and psychological enslavement into personal power. Snowy owl carries messages from the elders, and people with this bird as a totem will channel this wisdom in some way for the benefit of the world, usually in the form of the written word.

### Connecting with Owl Medicine

Exploring the magical world is at the heart of owl's teaching, and she has always held primary guardianship over this domain. You will find it beneficial to study the owl's realm of the night. If you sit outside after the sun has set, the world seems like a completely different place, especially if you are away from the chaos of city life. Listen to all the sounds you have never heard before and revel in the stillness of everything around you. This will allow you to feel the energy of owl at its strongest. Spending time alone is also a necessity when connecting with owl. As a solitary bird, owl gains strength, wisdom, and power from the solace of an empty night. Walk slowly in your work with owl, for it is not a medicine that can be rushed. During your work with an owl totem, remember to keep quiet. You must fly silently with this bird if she is to impart her wisdom upon you.

## Hawk/Falcon

*medicine:* insight, vision, messenger of the gods, focus, intellect

*family:* Accipitridae (hawk); Falconidae (Falcon)

*diet:* carnivorous—small mammals, birds, reptiles

*habitat:* deserts, grasslands, coniferous and deciduous forests, agricultural fields, urban centers (depending upon genus)

Of all the birds of prey, I consider hawks and falcons to be the most accessible and adaptable to the modern human, with the exception of the peregrine falcon. While eagle and owl are very powerful in the wild and as spirit guides, they can be difficult to entice into your corner … so to speak.

Hawks and falcons are usually closer to human activity, and have been trained in falconry for hundreds of years. Hawks and falcons are very strong, very powerful solar birds with celebrated mythologies that span the entire globe. Reverence for the hawk and falcon species comes down to us from the sacred religion and culture of ancient Egypt, where many of their most important deities were falcon-headed. They are first and foremost considered sun and sky deities, renowned for their speed and hunting precision. The peregrine falcon reaches a diving speed of up to 280 mph, and will catch its prey in midair. As a totem, a hawk or a falcon teaches swift action and fast progress while keeping your mind focused on your goals. Their vision is keen, and they will teach you how to overcome distractions in order to keep you on the right path.

## Peregrine Falcon/Falcon

Anyone in need of being pushed from a rut should study the peregrine falcon. Once believed to build its nest in the heavens, it is the most evolved of all the falcons in the world with its distinctive size and its ability to hunt prey in midair. The peregrine, often termed the great white shark of the sky, has long been admired for its speed, precision, and superior skill. With a dive speed of up to 280 mph, he embodies swiftness like no other bird, and as a totem, indicates fast forward movement in your life and a mental precision that allows the attainment of ambitions and ideals. The Peregrine is also renowned for its mental acuity, which becomes an inexhaustible gift of its teachings.

As a spiritual entity, the falcon had very early beginnings. The ancient Egyptians who settled along the Nile river five thousand years ago brought with them a falcon god—*Heru*, or *Horu*—inspired by the peregrine falcon. It was the most celebrated bird in ancient Egypt, appearing in every aspect of religious life and mythology. The Egyptians believed that the sun went around according to his purpose, and that the falcon, already in flight before sunrise, actually brought forth the sun into each new day. Many falcons were actually mummified in the same tradition as important people of the empire, which was viewed as a sign of great respect.

The falcon embodies many mystical qualities. They inhabit isolated terrain and appear aloof to the world around them. This characteristic will become apparent in those who follow the falcon's path, and they will enjoy, even *require*, a lofty retreat from the human world before making a swift dive back to the earth again. If the peregrine falcon has come to you as a teacher, be prepared to move swiftly through the next phase of your personal growth. Goals are within reach, but precision and bold movement may be required to secure the desired outcome.

Another lesson of the peregrine falcon concerns being in control. Moving at high speeds requires great discipline for peregrine falcon people, as the fall from such tremendous heights can be devastating. Knowing when to leap is just as important as having the skills and courage to do so. Peregrine falcon teaches her human companion how to release inhibitions about taking bold action in life. This wisdom is about taking chances, and leaping forward to embrace our future when the timing is right. But the Peregrine is not careless, and will utilize its great mental agility to navigate a world that is always changing and uncertain.

## Hawk

I had the pleasure of watching hawks every day in the Alberta countryside where I used to live. They would perch alongside the highways on utility poles waiting for the gophers to pop up from their holes, or would occasionally fly right through my backyard in the hope of snapping up a songbird that visited the feeders every day. They can see *everything,* it seems, which makes them fantastic spiritual allies.

Hawk is considered a visionary in many cultural traditions, and is often a totem of those who have bold and original ideas. Those with a hawk totem have sharp minds and keen intellects, and are able to detect the slightest movements of energy around them. Many hawk totem people have acute psychic abilities, and have mastered their inner vision by trusting what they see. Part of the visionary power of the hawk totem is using its power to help the world in some creative way. As a totem, hawk teaches us how to use our broad vision to find solutions to the world's problems. This is a great responsibility, and if the hawk has chosen you, it is time to act for the well-being of Mother Earth.

Most hawks are monogamous, taking another partner only if the original dies. There is a deep sense of loyalty within the hawk totem person that cherishes its close relationships to the fullest. The hawk as a totem will also be a loyal companion and teacher. Once it comes to you as a guide, it will remain with you for life, sharing its power and vision with you in every facet of life.

The red-tailed hawk, with its stunning red tail feathers, carries the added lesson of dealing with the rise of kundalini energy—the force that carries the flow of energy throughout the physical body. Only when the hawk has reached full maturation does he get these red feathers. Likewise, red-tailed hawk people must reach a certain level of maturity before earning the right to wield this power.

## Connecting with Hawk/Falcon Medicine

The hawk and the falcon are renowned for their excellent mental abilities. When you begin spiritual work with either of these birds, meditation will enhance your mental acuity, allowing greater focus and concentration. These are both very important attributes of hawk and falcon medicine, and must be worked upon if you are to gain the heightened perspective of these birds. The hawk and the falcon are also excellent companions when increasing your intuitive abilities due to their keen vision. Learning to respond to your inner visions in the physical world is likewise something you will develop as you grow in hawk/falcon wisdom, as well as your ability to trust in that which you see.

Birds of
the Water

Watching birds swim upon the waters is a peaceful and meditative pastime. They appear to be moving at the will of the currents, hiding the forces of their power below. You might say this is a metaphor for their teachings—being steady and calm on the outside, while directing their energy from within. They are unique in their spiritual contributions, and have always been important allies for shamans and magicians because of their mastery of the air, water, and earth simultaneously. Being symbolic of this elemental unity, they carry much ancient wisdom within the old pagan traditions.

Because water is associated with intuitive and emotional energy, water birds are often summoned for the healing of emotional imbalances and as aids when delving into the subconscious mind. If a water bird appears as a totemic ally, consider your current emotional life and how *you* are affecting your future with your current feelings and thought processes. This may also be a time of increased intuitive sensitivity and the awareness of other planes of existence.

## Swan

*medicine:* beauty, love, clairvoyance, serenity

*family:* Anatidae

*diet:* herbivorous—roots, stems, and leaves of submerged plants

*habitat:* freshwater and estuarine wetlands, flooded fields

As a poet and an author, the swan is very close to me as my creative muse. I keep swan feathers close by when writing, and know many artists of differing genres who do the same for a gentle touch of otherworldly inspiration. There is simply no other bird that seems to conjure up magical imagery as the swan does, filling the human imagination with scenes of beauty, grace, and romantic idealism. Swans radiate an otherworldly essence, almost dreamlike in their appearance. They are images of natural serenity as they glide effortlessly across the water's surface, and are the largest of all the aquatic birds. The trumpeter swan, having a wingspan of up to 96 inches and weighing up to 30 pounds, is nothing short of impressive. But aside from their obvious beauty, swans are known for their relatively long life span, twenty years in the wild, and up to around fifty years in captivity. They are also monogamous, thus having much to teach about loyalty and devotion.

In many cultures, the swan has been respected as a symbol of love, and in Celtic lore represented the sorrows of love and the affairs of the heart. It is not surprising to see the swan as a companion of Aphrodite, the goddess of romantic and erotic love and feminine beauty in ancient Greek mythology. Swans are very enigmatic beings and carry much sought-after energies. Many clairvoyants have close ties with the swan, as do poets and writers with a heightened receptivity to the undercurrents of the universe. Swans are the birds of the muses in Greek mythology, and in earlier times swans were believed to house the souls of poets. Shakespeare himself was called "the sweet swan of Avon." Swans are also believed to house the souls of great musicians, and Apollo's soul took the form of a swan in many Roman myths.

Swans appear often in Celtic symbolism, and have a familiar presence in Celtic iconography, appearing in a number of sculptures and ritual objects dating back to 1500 BCE. Swans were usually believed to be faeries in disguise in Celtic folklore, who preferred this bird form to any other for its otherworldly qualities. Swan goddesses and faeries of the Celtic tradition were famed for their wonderful voices and healing powers. They were identifiable from other swans by the gold and silver chains around their necks. Swans have been considered oracular birds for many centuries, but the ancient Celts seem to have had the greatest belief in the natural powers of this bird. They were also believed to carry the souls of Celtic chieftains to the afterlife. The following excerpt from "Omen of the Swans" (a Scottish Gaelic rendition) manifests the magnificent quality of the swan symbol and demonstrates the often idealized image of the bird:

I heard the sweet voice of the swans at the parting of day and night, gurgling on journeying wings putting forth their strength on high. I immediately stood still, I made no movement. I looked to see who was guiding in front, the Queen of Fortune, the white swan.[21]

In the lore of India, it was the swan who laid the Cosmic Egg upon the waters from which came forth Brahma, the supreme deity. Brahma's wife Saraswati—the goddess of wisdom, music, and learning, rode atop the swan as her preferred vehicle.[22]

---

21. Taken from *Lady of the Beasts* by Buffie Johnson (Inner Traditions, Rochester, VT), 77–7

22. See chapter 1, section 1 *Saraswati*, detailing the swan symbolism of this goddess

The Tlingit shamans of the Canadian Arctic considered swans to be their doctors, and the feet, neck, and heads of swans were used as containers for the ceremonial swans-down that was an essential component of a shaman's equipment.

In earlier pagan traditions the role of the swan in rituals was often not clearly distinguishable from that of the goose and the duck, as the symbolic characters of the three birds appear to have been interchangeable. In terms of spiritual symbolism, these three water birds carry many of the same attributes, particularly their affiliation with intuitive powers and emotional sensitivity. Swan medicine personifies grace, intuition, clairvoyance, and beauty. Because the swan floats gently upon the water, it is closely connected to our deep emotional and intuitive natures. Because water is influenced heavily by the powers of the moon, the swan has become a powerful feminine symbol. As a guide, the swan will naturally enhance creativity and psychic abilities in those who open themselves up freely to the bird's ancient wisdom.

Swans also possess shape-shifting abilities, transforming into people and back again in myths the world over. Many shamans wear swan feathers for their magical powers and their close connection to the spirit realms. Many otherworldly beings such as faeries, nymphs, and other spirits who wish to inhabit the earth in physical form choose this bird. Those with swan medicine will have a unique connection with the spirit world, experiencing its inhabitants in many curious ways. If you have a swan totem, you will be able to perceive altered states of awareness, and will have a strong connection to the underworld of the human psyche, exploring its many depths and peculiarities.

## Connecting with Swan Medicine

Water is an important aspect of swan's wisdom. Absorbing the energy of water enhances our emotional and intuitive natures. To better connect with swan, increase the amount of time you spend in water by taking frequent baths, or spending time near an ocean, lake, river, or pond. Listen to the harmonic sounds of the tides, or the gentle rushing of water over the rocks. Finding ways to balance and release the emotions is what swan medicine strives to achieve. Many people find singing an excellent way of expressing emotional energies. Legends say that the swan would sing a song before taking its final breath (the swan song). Singing brings us into harmony with our spiritual nature and is a wonderful way to express deep emotions. One can almost hear the ethereal voice of spirit at the sight of this magnificent bird. Writing poetry is likewise an emotional release. The swan is a bird of the muses, inspiring great words and poetic ideas. Receptivity is another important aspect of swan medicine. If you have a swan feather, make a quill pen from it to further enhance this connection.

## Loon

*medicine:* dreams, tranquility, wilderness, solitude

*family:* Gaviidae

*diet:* fish, amphibians, crustaceans

*habitat:* spends most of their time on the water

If swan conjures romantic idealism, then the loon represents the mysterious abyss from which our ideals are made. She often seems a lonely bird, gliding through the vast oceans of time in peace, reflection, and solace. The call of the loon is perhaps one of the most recognizable sounds of the wilderness, and is nothing short of haunting, enticing, and impenetrable. Loon is the summons to the realm of dreams and wishes, awakening those things that lay dormant below the surface of conscious awareness. Thoughts, talents, hopes, and ideals that endlessly seek fulfillment are the domain of loon, and through this water bird they find their expression in three dimensional reality.

Loon is a bird of great solitude and an enduring symbol of the wilderness. It is a bird highly respected in many native tribes for its knowledge of various earthly and otherworldly realms. When you daydream, that is loon medicine expanding your sphere of imagination. Although goose and swan are important creative allies, I often utilize loon magic when conjuring up children's stories, like fantasies, because loon stirs the images of lost realms and spaces. I enjoy the ways the spirit of loon makes things appear in my mind's eye, dangling strange and wonderful pictures in front of me.

Loon medicine connects us to nature, and reminds us to keep our relationship to the Earth Mother strong and enduring. If the loon is drawing your attention to her mysterious calls, it may be time to escape the machine-oriented world and reconnect with the spirit of the wild.

The loon, often called a diver, catches its food by swimming calmly along the water's surface, and then plunging abruptly into the water. People with this bird totem are able to delve deep into the psyche to retrieve latent powers, hidden emotions, and sometimes even past-life memories.

This is a wonderful ability that will aid in healing old pains and bringing forgotten strengths and powers to the surface. People who carry loon medicine often have vivid visions that can be difficult to separate from the present dimension. Loon medicine is somewhat ethereal, always bringing to the waking mind a dream-like world to decipher and somehow show the world.

The loon is an excellent swimmer, but fares rather poorly on land. This may be a problem for the person with loon as a totem, as their attention to the world of dreams and emotions may make it difficult to focus in everyday life. Coming back to the surface often takes more skill than being able to dive to the depths in the first place.

The loon, being a diving bird, is closely connected to the underwater realms that symbolize the subconscious mind. This is where we store the things of the imagination—daydreams, hopes, secret wishes, artistic ideas, and fairy-tales, which all brim to the top with loon medicine. Loon carries the medicine of creation and imagination, and is a helpful ally when undertaking lucid dreaming. It will arrive as a totem animal when we need to bring hidden dreams and talents to the surface, and will encourage the full acceptance and expression of those things long buried. When we neglect our most profound dreams, they will haunt us forever—this is the call of loon.

Diving birds have always held a special place in shamanic traditions, having contact with entities from the lower regions. Their ability to dive to great depths—as much as 240 feet below the surface—is due to their solid bones, an attribute that gives the loon a great distinction. All other birds have hollow bones, and could not venture as deep as the loon. The loon spends most of its time in the water, and, because of this, is often called the "Rain Goose," and, in many cultures heralds the coming of rain.

## Connecting with Loon Medicine

To connect with this mysterious water bird, spend time in quiet, lonely places. The loon inhabits peaceful waters; take time to understand the magic of the silence and solitude that loon embodies. Within this silence, allow your dreams to unfold in your mind. Play out your heart's desires and wishes to unlock your hidden feelings. Pay close attention to your visions and dreams. Start a journal during your work with this bird, as you will no doubt have some very interesting inner experiences. Loon medicine is also a call of the wilderness. It is one of the enduring symbols of the natural world and the escape from modern life. Enhance your experience with loon by taking an outdoor retreat. Canoeing on a quiet lake would be an ideal way to understand this bird's peaceful quality.

# Heron

*medicine:* self-reliance, introspection

*family:* Ardeidae

*diet:* frogs, rabbits, small birds, fish and other aquatic species

*habitat:* freshwater marshes, saltwater marshes, swamps, flooded meadows, shorelines, and lakes

The inscription above the ancient oracle at Delphi, "Know Thyself," is the essence of the heron's wisdom. It is a powerful totem, carrying the knowledge of independence and learning how to stand on your own. I have been lucky to observe many blue herons near my home on Vancouver Island. One even let me sit about two feet away as he stood on the shoreline peacefully watching the waters. Their patience, strength, and size are all equally magnificent.

The heron is an ancient bird with fascinating mythological associations. It was the bird used in ancient Egypt to represent the mythical Benu, and was believed to be the creator of light, both here and in ancient Wales. This large water bird was also considered to be the emblem of the lost city of Atlantis. In Greek legend the bird was sacred to Poseidon, god of the sea, and the people of Atlantis were said to be his children.

Heron teaches us how to explore the depths of our experience. Its classic one-legged pose has made it a symbol of contentment, contemplation, and the state of meditation— all of which are crucial in the process of self-reflection. In Native American lore, deceased wise men are said to return to the earth as herons.

The heron is an ambush predator, waiting still in the water until its prey is within striking distance. As a spirit guide it will naturally teach the power of being still until proper action is required. It is a bird of balance, inner harmony, and poise, with a quiet air of unpretentious pride. It is a solitary bird, gathering in colonies only for the purposes of mating and raising the young, and people with this medicine often find it hard to maintain long-term relationships.

When within the colony, however, the heron exudes peace and cooperation, teaching the same lesson to those it visits as a totem.

The heron exhibits its greatest attributes when left to its hermit-like nature, quietly observing the world around it. Herons are the monks of the bird world, and as such emanate an intelligent self-awareness that surpasses the average individual. Those on the path of this bird are very reflective by nature, and will relish those times when they can retreat from the business of the world to the solitude of their lonely nest.

Heron medicine involves knowing the self above everything else. It is the ability to look inside of our emotions, actions, and thoughts for the truth behind them. Heron people have always been able to do this as an inherent part of their nature. If this great bird comes as a totem, then you are being asked to learn this essential skill at this time. Heron asks you not only to know yourself from the very depths of your being, but also to trust yourself and your path; there is no room for doubt in the process of transformation and evolution.

## Connecting with Heron Medicine

Those working with a heron totem would benefit greatly from the ancient practice of meditation. This will allow you to achieve the inner poise and stillness of the heron, and connect with its natural qualities of balance and harmony. Write down your thoughts, emotions, and revelations during your meditative work in order to chart your progress. Yoga will likewise enhance your work with heron. Yoga poses encourage focus and concentration and would be an excellent way to connect with the stillness that this great bird exudes.

## Pelican

*medicine:* self-sacrifice, devotion

*family:* Pelecanidae

*diet:* fish, amphibians, crustaceans

*habitat:* coastal areas, beaches, lagoons

Another large, interesting water bird is the pelican, which boasts an impressive pouched bill and stunning wingspan. The largest pelican, believed to be the Dalmatian pelican, has a wingspan of up to 11.5 feet.

Pelicans are excellent swimmers, giving them a culturally significant connection with the water. The brown pelican is a plunge diver, dropping from the air at 37 mph into the water to catch its prey. This is often used as a metaphor for the ability to tap into hidden resources that lie below the visible surface of awareness. Pelicans usually fish in groups, being very community oriented and working as a team to catch their meals. An important aspect of this bird's medicine is being able to cooperate with the whole in order to survive. The pelican will choose to work with those whose intentions are always about positively impacting the world as a whole.

Most of the mythology surrounding this bird comes down to us from very old and very unique beliefs. Legends say that the pelican would pierce its own chest in order to nourish its young during times of famine. Another story describes a pelican who killed her young and, out of terrible grief, gave them her blood to resurrect them. These stories, although having no basis in reality, gave rise to the pelican as a symbol of Christ and his suffering for the nourishment of others. The pelican's habit of resting its long bill on its chest, and the appearance of the red pouch on the Dalmatian Pelican early on in the breeding season, had no doubt contributed to the mythologies of the past. A mother pelican, regurgitating food for her young, unavoidably drops blood on her chest while feeding from her long bill, which is another tangible explanation for the wealth of folklore surrounding this great bird.

The pelican is believed to have mysterious life-giving powers, and is linked with the alchemical process of resurrection like the phoenix. It is a nurturing mother, and, because of its mythological past, is a worldwide symbol of charity, compassion, and devotion to others. Queen Elizabeth wore a pendant depicting a pelican, representing her selfless love of her people. If pelican has chosen you as a student, you are being asked to look at *your* devotion, either to your goals, your children, your partner or religion, or to the world at large. It is time to put your heart into selfless giving, and nurture some area of your life that has been neglected. Pelican may also be drawing attention to your devotion to yourself. Giving selflessly must be balanced with accepting nourishment in return from others and from the gifts given by the universe every day.

The pelican also carries the medicine of buoyancy, being able to pop up to the surface after plunging beneath the water. Air sacs in the neck and breast make this bird un-sinkable. This is highly symbolic for those carrying pelican medicine, and will indicate the ability to stay afloat even under the most strenuous and difficult of life's situations. There is a natural lightness inherent in pelican medicine that enables a life-long endurance. The lives of Mother Teresa and Gandhi come to mind when relating the message of the pelican totem, and serve as reminders of just how exceptional self-sacrifice is in the world of ego.

Charity is at the heart of this bird's wisdom, and is often a critical lesson when walking the ways of spirit. Learning to give of oneself is a lost art in the modern world, but is a very ancient teaching embodied in the behavior of the pelican. Family is another aspect of this wisdom. Spend more time with family and friends, giving your attention and love freely. Notice how the dynamics within your family change when you factor in some extra quality time. It may be a time to nurture your personal relationships within your home and family unit.

### Connecting with Pelican Medicine

Being symbolic of the compassionate side of human nature, truly understanding Pelican's meaning will require a self-less contribution on your part. You don't need to become a martyr to experience this bird's ancient teachings, but giving for the sake of others will help you see how extraordinary it is to act in accordance with spirit, rather than ego. There are very few people today who can live their entire lives with this foundation. To see the Pelican's great nurturing qualities, and work them into your own life, ensure a healthy balance of giving to yourself, and giving to the whole world."

# Kingfisher

*medicine:* prosperity, new experiences, agility
*families:* Alcedinidae, Halcyonidae, Cerylidae
*diet:* fish, crayfish, frogs, insects, other reptiles
*habitat:* woodlands and wetlands

Kingfishers are small, brightly colored birds with large heads and long pointed bills. They are patient, agile, and very quick when diving into the water, and have long been symbols of prosperity and abundance. The kingfisher has an interesting mythology that traces back to the days of ancient Greece. In the Greek myth, Alcyone (daughter of the king of the winds) found her husband drowned; out of devotion she cast herself into the sea. The gods rewarded her action by turning her into a kingfisher, and her father forbade the winds to blow during the incubation period of these birds. These fourteen days—the seven prior to and following the winter solstice—were called the *Halcyon Days*. And so the ancients believed that the kingfisher had the power to calm the sea in order to nest upon it.

In China, the plumage of the kingfisher is said to vie in color with the sky and the blue-green of the distant hills. The iridescent feathers of the kingfisher were once used by Chinese artisans to decorate hair and clothing accessories, such as hairpins and brooches, thus giving rise to the king-fisher as a symbol of feminine beauty. This belief may also come from the fact that the female, and not the male, has more color on her feathers, something not typically seen in the bird world.

The kookaburra, the largest member of the kingfisher family, is well known for its uncanny laughter, echoing that of a human's. This cackling is done at the hours of dusk and dawn in order to mark the bird's territory. It is also an excellent diver—but in the air instead of the water. They will swoop down rapidly upon their prey, not giving it the chance to get away. This can easily be applied to your life and how you go after what you desire.

The kookaburra also has a family life distinct from the other kingfishers. When the young have matured, they will stay in the nest to help raise the parent's second brood. This is an extremely rare occurrence in nature, and reflects the birds' teaching of family unity and cooperation.

Kingfishers have very keen vision, both in the air and while swimming underwater, thus gaining a mastery of both realms. They are solitary birds, and will often tunnel into sand banks several feet deep. The medicine of the kingfisher imparts a great need for personal space and the need to spend time with one's inner thoughts and emotions. As rapid divers, kingfishers jump headlong into the waters to find prey. The person with a kingfisher totem likewise will dive into the waters of life without fear or hesitation. This may be the lesson brought to you by a kingfisher totem, and there will no doubt be many new experiences entering your life that will afford you the opportunity for uninhibited exploration.

## Connecting with Kingfisher Medicine

For those with a kingfisher totem, the diving behavior of this bird will be very symbolic. In shamanic terms, the diving from the air to the underwater world represents the journey of the shaman from the upper worlds to the underworld and back to earth again. Spending time in or around water is an important way of connecting with the powers of the kingfisher. Try diving from high places, as into a swimming pool, in imitation of this bird. This is a wonderful way to experience the diving skills of the kingfisher that are a critical part of its survival and shamanic qualities. This exercise will allow you to feel the impact of abruptly going from one realm to another.

## Penguin

*medicine:* sacrifice, endurance, dreams

*family:* Spheniscidae

*diet:* krill, fish, squid

*habitat:* cold arctic regions

Penguins are truly amazing aquatic birds. I view them as the great warriors of the avian world, being well equipped to endure perils that many others could not even fathom. Penguins face a lot of hardship in their cold, unforgiving habitat, and are the generous teachers of fortitude, strength, and acceptance. If I could pick and choose my totems personally, I would choose the penguin for these unique strengths, its group-mindedness, and ability to fight through difficulty with balance and calm. They are wonderful allies for serious spiritual work involving hard life lessons.

Penguins are aquatic, flightless birds that are extremely well adapted to life in the water. They spend half of their lives in the ocean, and so carry powerful teachings about our emotional natures and dreaming minds. The Emperor penguin, being the largest species of this bird, measures approximately 3 feet, 7 inches tall. Some prehistoric penguins reached enormous heights, averaging the size of an adult human. The smallest penguin, the Little Blue Penguin, measures only 16 inches. The larger penguins generally live in the colder climates, while the smaller species inhabit moderate climates in the southern hemisphere. The vestigial wings of the penguin have become flippers through evolutionary processes. This allows them a supreme adaptation to aquatic life, which they have mastered like no other bird.

Penguins are usually gentle birds, not having developed any real fear of humankind. Because they have no land predators, they are more trusting than other birds, although they will always exercise caution during any encounter—keeping a distance of around 3 meters from contact. When working with a penguin as a guide, you will naturally be very trusting. Although this may be a necessary lesson for some, it can be a caution for others who forget to put up boundaries in social situations.

Penguins are very vocal birds, and have developed a high level of social interaction living in very large colonies together. People with this bird ally will thrive in places with large amounts of people where a sense of brotherhood, or sisterhood, is maintained. Penguin will also impart on its human companion the ability to maintain strong connections to a wide group of friends and family, keeping the penguin totem person amid the social intricacies of both.

These birds are wonders to people who encounter them in the wild. They have adapted to the harshest environments in the world where many others would soon perish. They are able to survive the coldest temperatures, which underlines another important lesson of this bird—that of endurance. Those with a penguin totem will be faced with many challenges in life. It must be remembered that these lessons come to us for our own personal growth and should be accepted with humility and strength. Penguin is a powerful guide through the icy winters of life, and will gift you with all that you need to survive and thrive in any circumstance. Penguin has made a haven out of the coldest of places and he will teach you how to do the same.

The black and white coloring, although very symbolic for the penguin totem person, serves as a camouflage in the waters it inhabits. The natural predators of the penguin— the Orca and the leopard seal—have difficulty distinguishing the white belly of the bird from the waters reflective surface. Their black coloring on the back keeps them camouflaged from an aerial view. This black and white plumage represents the perfect balance between light and dark, male and female, and in nature both the male and the female share in the care of the eggs, and are both very caring and protective of their young.

Like many other water birds, penguins are great divers, reaching a diving speed of up to 16.8 mph. They are very agile underwater, and carry the lessons associated with dreaming and astral travel. They are masters of the hidden underworld realms, making them wonderful shamanic allies for spiritual journeying. People with a penguin spirit guide are often vivid dreamers and are able to slip into alternate states of awareness quite rapidly, having learned to balance many realities at once.

## Connecting with Penguin Medicine

The penguin has a special connection to the water. Explore this natural environment of the penguin to form a bond between you and their underwater world. Spending greater amounts of time in the water will also enhance your ability to move back and forth between the physical world and that of the subconscious mind. Penguin also governs the realm of dream work. As a master of the unconscious, penguin will show you how to navigate and control the dream world. Keep a journal of your dreams and visions while working with a penguin totem.

# Stork

*medicine:* fertility, family dynamics, ancestry

*family:* Ciconiidae

*diet:* frogs, insects, small birds, lizards, rodents

*habitat:* open farmland, marshy wetlands

The stork has an interesting mythology, conjuring up images of familial unity and fertility. Who doesn't remember the story of babies being delivered by storks when our parents really didn't want to discuss the "birds and the bees." It is one of those archetypes that has secured its position in our minds and imaginations for decades.

The stork is a wading bird, standing 40–50 inches tall, with a 69–71-inch wingspan. They have long been considered emblems of parental care, and have been observed for centuries in their nests (often close to human habitations themselves). The stork family includes herons, egrets, ibises, and spoonbills, which should all be studied closely for their similar qualities and mythological associations.

They are symbols of fertility and the return of spring, and are strongly connected to the family as loving, nurturing parents. Stork medicine embodies changes in family dynamics and the structure of the family unit as a whole. If stork has come as a spirit guide, the energies of family and home will become of utmost concern to you. The stork will return to the same nesting site every year, which expresses a heartfelt loyalty to the home. This bird may portend a time of reconnecting with your ancestral roots and the foundations of your family structure.

The stork has no means of vocal communication, using bill clapping, body gestures, and dance instead. As a spirit guide and teacher, stork will show you how to use your actions to communicate your thoughts and feelings. It is a time to express your truth through the things that you do rather than what you say. If you are a parent this should be reflected in the examples you set for your children. The stork holds the ancient knowledge of sacred fertility dances, and reminds us that we all have the power to dance our truest desires into creation, a lesson also seen in the teachings of the grouse. You may need to look at alternative methods of strengthening your physical body by means of dance and/or yoga practices.

The stork is usually viewed as a symbol of good luck, and represents a life-long commitment to familial values. In ancient Egypt the stork symbolized the *ba*, which was the unique character of every human being, or the soul. The old legend of the stork bringing babies comes from several ancient beliefs. It may be the old beliefs among the ancients that the souls of the unborn waited in ponds and marshes until their birth. Storks, being wading birds, were a natural choice as the bringers of new babies out of the waters of life. Another possible explanation for the myth is that many stork species nest so close to human habitation, sometimes on the top of chimneys.

In ancient Greece, the stork was associated with the goddess Hera as the protector of nursing mothers, and Aristotle reported that it was a devastating crime to kill this bird. The stork was shown as the vehicle of the god Hermes in art, and was often portrayed as killing snakes. This symbolism continued into Christian times, where the stork was viewed as the destroyer of evil personified by the snake. Later Christian iconographers associated the stork with piety, purity, and resurrection. In the Orient, the stork is an enduring symbol of longevity, and the Taoists use this bird to represent immortality.

### Connecting with Stork Medicine

The stork is another bird that encourages familial bonding. Being more attentive to those you love, whether your children, pets, or parents, will bring you closer to the stork's ancient wisdom of the importance of a healthy home life. This bird's wisdom will teach you your own role within the family unit, and will extend this knowledge out into the world family as a whole. With stork medicine, your abilities to nurture and give to the world will become paramount.

# Goose

*medicine:* spiritual journeying, eloquence with words, connection to the archetypal world

*family:* Anatidae

*diet:* grassy plants, leaves, flowers, stems, roots, seeds, and berries

*habitat:* wetlands, wet grassy meadows, ponds, and lakes

The goose is one of my favorite birds. When I lived in Alberta I had the esteemed privilege of seeing hundreds every year as they departed and returned at the whims of mother nature. I remember a spring morning when a Canada goose wandered into my backyard, picking at the seeds I had put out for the songbirds—not exactly what I was expecting, but fantastic nonetheless!

What I enjoy most about Canada geese is their instinctual need to migrate, as if their very souls drive them onward to new and wonderful adventures. Nature makes them restless when it is time to move, a response we humans could make better use of. Goose teaches the need to follow the whims, desires, and restless pacings of the heart. Like the loon, the goose inspires imaginary worlds and things that need to be brought into being. It is the bird of writers, and those wanderers in spirit and untamed in heart. I actually keep a giant goose garden statue on each side of my computer desk as a gentle reminder to keep pushing the boundaries and conventions of the written word.

The goose is nothing short of impressive, measuring 30–43 inches long with a 50–71-inch wingspan on the Canada goose. It is a frequent mythological entity, and has been connected with folklore, goddess mythology, and the matriarchal archetype since the days of ancient Egypt. In the mythology from this culture, the goddess Hathor gave birth to the sun when she took the form of the Nile goose, which was later translated into the "goose that laid the golden egg." The goose remained sacred to Celtic tribes because of its connection to the sun-egg, and it was forbidden to kill a goose in midwinter during medieval times because it was thought that the goose brought forth the sun again in the spring. The goose was held as a sacred bird in Rome at the temple of Juno. Legend tells us that the geese living at the temple alerted the Romans to intruding Gauls, thus saving the city. From that point on, the birds were allowed to live out their lives under the protection of the great deity, and thereafter were symbols of vigilance and protection.

Goose medicine connects us to the stories of the past, and allows us to find solace in the threads that connect the human race over many centuries and cultures via folktales and myths. These stories present the archetypal images and common quests of people everywhere, and will always tie past, present, and future together. It is not surprising that *Mother Goose* became the personification of story-time, and that her imagery has interesting associations with earlier pagan mythologies. There are many visual references of *Mother Goose* that allude to her possible beginnings as a bird goddess, such as the half-bird, half-woman guise, or the several images of the old woman riding on the back of a goose. This image was widely seen throughout the ancient world with Aphrodite, Saraswati, and several other bird deities.

Goose medicine is strong in writers, as this great bird imparts the gift of the written word and a deep appreciation of human language. Many writers will use a goose feather quill pen when in need of inspiration. Goose medicine teaches the importance of allowing our inner voice to guide us through life, and often appears to those who have forgotten the inherent gift of intuition that we each possess.

Geese mate for life, signaling a highly developed sense of loyalty and devotion. Family bonds are very strong among Canada geese. The young will stay with their parents for an entire year, returning to the breeding grounds with them again after their first winter. A person with goose medicine will have a strong sense of family duty, and will usually stay very close with their family well into their adult years. Geese are masters of navigation, and they use their strong instinctual abilities to migrate every year. The Canada goose can travel up to 621.4 miles a day. This has made the goose a symbol for the great quests of the spiritual warrior, and beckons those it visits on toward great adventures of the spirit. If the goose has entered your life as a totem, it is a summons to begin a journey of some kind. There are often many spiritual lessons inorporated in the flight of the goose that will propel you forward in awareness.

### Connecting with Goose Medicine

Goose holds the power to connect the past, present, and future experiences that all of humanity shares. It is the herald of the hero quest, and the spiritual journeys everyone must go through on the earth plane. To bring the power of this bird into your life, write about your own spiritual quest in the form of a story—linking your experiences to those throughout history. Try to find the common threads between the hero myths of the past and your own life journey. If goose is your personal medicine, your power is the power of words. Use them to create those fabulous realities that have inspired the world from the beginning of humankind.

## Flamingo

*medicine:* community, dance, leisure

*family:* Phoenicopteriformes

*diet:* brine shrimp

*habitat:* alkaline or saline lakes, mangrove swamps, tidal flats, sandy islands

The flamingo is an interesting bird to study, and an even more interesting one to watch. The example of the flamingo dance (p. 41) is a great indication of their sense of community and leisure, and is how they stay connected with their group over a lifetime. Although the dances appear somewhat strange, it is one of the most breathtaking sights in the world. Flamingo medicine also involves using dance as a way of connecting with and expressing the life force.

Another attribute that separates this bird from others is its characteristic pink coloring. In nature this is caused by the beta carotene in their diet. When absent, their feathers will turn pure white. This ability to change color reflects some of their medicine qualities—that of illusion and shape shifting. Flamingo totem people make excellent actors and performers of all types, and are good at pretending to be what they are not. The pink coloring is also symbolic of the love they feel for their community. Because they live in large flocks, they have a strong sense of security. They are seldom seen alone and often have great difficulty just *being* on their own. They are followers in every sense of the word and will reflect similar tendencies of groupmindedness in the person carrying their medicine.

Flamingos mate for life and are very loyal to their partners. They are sociable, vocal, and will teach those with this totem how to live in harmony with the beings with whom they share the planet. The flamingo, and likewise flamingo-totem people, thrive in group settings, and rely on the vision of the group rather than on their own whimsical and uncharted ideas. Wonderful team players, flamingo people will dedicate themselves to helping organizations that benefit humanity as a whole.

The flamingo's migratory travels cover greater distances than most other birds, and it is often seen as a symbol of leisure. In ancient Egypt, the flamingo represented the hieroglyph for the color red, and was another symbol of the sun god Ra. Because the Flamingo lives on hot volcanic lakes, it has been connected to the legendary phoenix. The word *flamingo* derives from *flamenco*, a word that itself derives from the Latin word *flame*.

If the flamingo has come to you as a totem, it may be a time of connecting with the world at large. It means that your energies and skills will be best used for the benefit of the whole community, and not just for the purposes of individual success. Share what you have to offer with humanity, and become a groupminded being who can bring people together in meaningful ways.

## *Connecting with Flamingo Medicine*

The flamingo thrives in large group settings. It is a bird of community, and is unable to work as an independent being. You may need to look at the ways you involve yourself in the world around you. Some people are born solitaries, but most require a thriving social network to survive. To connect with this bird's wisdom, join organizations that allow you to work *with* groups of people. This will instill the sense of groupmindedness that the flamingo totem wishes to teach you. The flamingo uses dance to enhance the social relationships within the group. You may find it helpful to explore some kind of dancing that encourages merging and dancing in unison with others. This is always an enriching experience for those working with a flamingo guide.

## Crane

*medicine:* independence, love, loyalty

*family:* Gruidae

*diet:* omnivorous—crustaceans, fish, insects, plants

*habitat:* marshes, shallow ponds, small creeks, wetlands

The crane is a very ancient bird, with much wisdom to offer humankind. Whooping cranes have been gracing planet earth for an estimated 3.5 million years. Included in this bird's medicine are the lessons of communication, love, community, longevity, and independence. Many ancient cultures saw parallels with the crane and humanity, such as longevity of life, the tendency for monogamous relationships, and the strong sense of community and social cohesiveness displayed by the crane species.

This group mindedness of the crane has been admired most notably in Asian traditions, where people still live within the larger family and community units. Those working with crane may need to observe their own relationships with the world around them. Crane people must learn to be a part of their community, or even the earth at large, while still maintaining their unique viewpoints and dreams within that whole.

Because they mate for life, cranes have long been symbols of love and fertility. Crane imagery still adorns many Asian residences for this ancient symbolism, and cranes are often depicted as pairs to represent perfect love in the Feng Shui tradition.

An impressive behavior of the crane species is the unison call, which allows a pair of cranes to connect both emotionally and physiologically. This complex duet helps the pair reinforce their bond with each other, and also serves as a territorial warning for other cranes. Each crane pair has a unique and distinguishable call from other pairs, which allows for easy recognition in the wild. As a totem, the crane is a wonderful teacher of proper communication between pairs, whether romantic or otherwise. Vocalization is a very important aspect of this bird's medicine.

In nature, a crane may spontaneously break into dance, which then spreads like wildfire throughout the entire flock. They also dance to release tension when disturbed or angry, to thwart aggression, to distract predators, and to advertise occupation of territory. Sometimes, however, cranes dance for what appears to be no reason at all. Captive cranes dance in fine weather, and penned birds dance when they are released from their enclosures. The black-necked cranes in Central Bhutan are held in special esteem by the Buddhist monks. Each year, these birds leave the Tibetan Plateau to winter in Bhutan. The cranes arrive predictably on the same day every year, and, upon their arrival, will fly three times around the ancient Gantey Gompa monastery. This miraculous behavior is echoed by the Buddhist monks who walk three times around a shrine when they arrive at a sacred place.

Cranes are blessed with a natural beauty and grace, and through human eyes we see their dances and songs as expressions of joy, devotion, and the eternal anticipation of finding one's soul mate. Among the Ojibwa, people of the crane clan have traditionally been honored as tribal leaders. In ancient Greek and Roman legends, it was the crane who inspired the letters of the alphabet with their unique flying formations. Ancient Egyptians worshiped a mythical sun-bird deity known as the B*enu,* depicted as a crane in their early cultural history. It is believed that the legendary phoenix was taken from these early descriptions of the B*enu,* probably due to its connection in later Egyptian history with Osiris, the god of death and resurrection. Cranes were often depicted in tombs and sacred temples.

In Chinese legend, sages were said to fly to Heaven if they rode on the backs of cranes, and a sage able to transform himself into a crane was believed to achieve immortality. In Imperial China, the image of a crane was embroidered on the robes of high officials, and statues of cranes flanked the emperor's throne in the Forbidden City of Beijing. In

Japan, the crane is called *Honorable Lord Crane*, and is the guardian of the Otherworld to the Celts. In ancient Rome, the author Martial and fifth-century statesman Flavius Cassiodous both declared that the entire Greek alphabet was obtained by Mercury, the messenger god, as he watched the flight of cranes.

In western Sweden rocks have been found adorned with images of crane dances, dating back roughly five millennia, and cranes are still celebrated there today as the harbingers of spring.

### Connecting with Crane Medicine

The crane is a joyful bird, able to express the innate rhythms of the universe. Dancing is the most important thing you can do to connect with this bird's very ancient wisdom. Allow yourself to find your own expression of nature's rhythms through your body. Yoga and ballet are among the most fluid forms of dancing for these purposes. As the crane will dance to release tension, you will likewise find peace and physical relaxation through dancing exercises. To try a shamanic dance of the crane, watch videos of these birds in action and imitate their sacred movements.

Songbirds

The melodious sounds of these avian creatures evoke eternal wonder within the human soul. Many species fall under the classification of songbird—among them finches, warblers, thrushes, buntings, and chickadees. A bird's song is a joy to the ear, but it is, in reality, a whole world of language impenetrable to our seemingly superior understanding.

Most songbirds have been regarded as symbols of regeneration and new beginnings from very early in human history. They return every spring as beacons of new life on earth after the harsh winter months, and promise a renewal of body, mind, and spirit. Songbirds were long connected with goddesses of fertility and love for their nurturing symbolism. The Celtic goddess of the moon, Rhiannon, was a protector of songbirds everywhere. Even today it is believed that feeding songbirds is a display of devotion to this great and powerful goddess. Songbirds are high-energy birds, buzzing and whirling in a multitude of directions. Some of them feed on the sweet nectar of flowers, like the hummingbird, to increase stamina prior to migration. They are messengers of communication, the joy of song and personal expression, and renewal after death and decay.

## Sparrow

*medicine:* self-worth, survival, assertiveness, trust

*family:* Passeridae

*diet:* seeds, nuts, berries, buds, insects

*habitat:* near human habitation, farms, forests, very widely distributed

I enjoy the multitudes of sparrows that visit my yard every day. They are fairly easy to please as long as you give them plenty of seed and fresh water. They are such social creatures, whirling about in giant flocks, crowding together at the bird bath, and mobbing a plentiful feeder. They personify the idea of strength in numbers by sticking together as a family unit.

The sparrow, however, is traditionally regarded as a bird of love, not society, and holds a sacred status with Aphrodite of ancient Greece. The Greek poet Sappho imagined Aphrodite's chariot to be drawn by sparrows in her "Hymn to Aphrodite." Sparrow is sometimes considered the natural romantic of the bird world, showering their mates with affection.

It is a bird of survival, assertiveness, and of understanding one's place in the world around us. It is a teacher of self-worth and dignity, showing us how to adapt to our current incarnation on the earth plane. We all have a place in the world and we must develop and utilize our talents for the good of the whole. Sparrow also teaches humility, compassion, and charity to those who become too self-consumed in their own affairs. This bird came to personify the lower classes (peasants) of Europe in the Middle Ages, who had no power against the stern authority of the rich and wealthy. It is also a common superstition that sparrows carry the souls of the dead.

The sparrow is a common bird, and continually asserts itself to the world, proving its sense of worth through its longevity and adaptability. It represents an exuberant spirit, joyful in its existence upon Mother Earth. It is cheerful and dramatic, its survival due in great part to its relationship with humans. Sparrows live close to the human world and are able to take advantage of shelter, food, and water that bird lover's everywhere share with their feathered friends. Sparrows are very sociable birds, taking every moment to enjoy the company of their own kind, and even of humans.

I had a close encounter with a sparrow last fall, that seemed lost or somehow separated from his usual company. The little house sparrow was stubbornly sitting in the parking lot of a car dealership, uninjured, but in danger of being run over. After a challenging rescue, I had managed to get the bird home when a bad storm began. The bird chose not to ride the storm out in the large pine outside my house, but rather insisted on staying indoors with me. It perched on my shoulder, ate seeds from my hand, groomed its feathers, and burrowed itself into my hair. After the storm, it ventured toward the tree, but kept a close eye on me—flying over to perch on my shoulder or sit in my hair every time it saw me outside. The fact that sparrows remain so close to people is how they ensure their survival, since many of the sparrow's natural predators will not venture near human-populated areas.

The sparrow is a lucky bird, and sparrow people know how to get whatever they need. Not by working too hard, but by an innate trust that what they really need is always right there for the taking. Sparrow knows he or she can trust the universe, because it will always take care of them. This will be one of the most crucial lessons of those with this totem: trusting that everything *will* be alright in the end.

## Connecting with Sparrow Medicine

Sparrow medicine involves recognizing your own self worth. Work on ways to become more assertive and express your confidence to the world. This might entail doing things that honor your well-being, like getting a massage or going shopping for yourself. A lack of self-love will only promote life experiences that reflect such a state of negativity. It has been said that we can never truly give love to others if we do not love ourselves first. It is important to remember your natural ability to receive the bounty of the universe and manifest joy in the simple life. When you do achieve your "bounty" from the universe, remember the joy of sharing what you have with those you love.

# Nightingale

*medicine:* poetry, song, love

*family:* Muscicapidae

*diet:* insects

*habitat:* forest areas

A bird of sweet musing, the nightingale has been held in high esteem by poets for centuries. John Keats called it the "light-winged Dryad of the trees,"[23] and it has long remained the muse of love and the power of poetry over the human heart. The song of the nightingale stands out to us because it is one of the few birds that sing at night. The nightingale passes the silence of the night with its captivating whistles

---

23. From *Ode to a Nightingale*

and trills, which are as enchanting to the human ear as the mysterious night calls of the owl.

The reputation of the nightingale as a mystical poet-singer has endured into modern times. It is a symbol for eloquence, inspiration, and poetic genius, and imprints these qualities upon the human who is aligned with its wisdom. It is considered a poet in the most profound sense of the word, and embodies in its song the thoughts and feelings of love in all of its depth.

The Anglo Saxon name *nightingale* means "night songstress," and the Spanish once called this bird *Ruisenor* ("king" or "master"). Although the female was once believed to be the songstress, it is actually the male that sings (which is often the case with many songbirds).

Nightingale is the messenger of love and of a new day rising. If the nightingale flies your way as a totem, you are being asked to sing the song in your heart in order to unleash your unique personal expression and truth. It is the appearance of inspiration and creativity. It is sometimes described as a shy bird, and this trait will likely be inherent in nightingale people. The nightingale's moonlight singing connects it to the cycles of the moon, and thus to the archetypal feminine energies and moon magic. It was also associated with the deities Adonis and Attis, being a part of their magical rites of the ancient world. Nightingale wisdom involves the opening of the heart to the night, and inspires the joyful expression of singing for the love of song.

*Connecting with Nightingale Medicine*

The nightingale is the muse of poetic inspiration. Writing can be a very cathartic practice, allowing thoughts and feeling to stream forth from your subconscious. If you are working with the nightingale as a totem, or would just like to connect more strongly with the ancient art of the poets, studying poetry and working on your own style will enhance your experience of this bird's wisdom. As another bird encouraging the medicine of song, it is an excellent teacher in the methods of clearing your throat with the power of song. Your voice is more powerful than you think. The nightingale will show you how to use it to manifest what is in your heart.

# Chickadee

*medicine:* bravery, boldness, truth, unity

*family:* Paridae

*diet:* insects, seeds, berries

*habitat:* mixed or deciduous woods, urban areas

I must admit I have an unfair bias toward the chickadee. They personify simplistic beauty to me, and they are just delightful to observe in the wild. They love to eat seeds and donuts, and will sing their melody back and forth to each other all day long. Because they are native to North America, there is a limited mythological background for this bold little bird. Chickadee has been a very important bird for the Native Indian tribes of North America, however, and is still highly regarded as a symbol of truth and bravery. The

Cherokee believe that a person with a chickadee totem will not tell a lie, as it is a bird of the highest expression of truth. They are bold and inquisitive little birds, and often amaze people by landing near, and sometimes on, humans, and even cats! They seem to have a natural ability to discern real danger, giving them an inherent understanding of the truth behind every situation. Like the chickadee, people working with its wisdom must embrace their lives without fear, distinguishing *real* challenges from presumed dangers.

When a chickadee is challenged by a larger bird, it will stand fearless in defense of itself and its territory. Although a small bird, it carries a powerful medicine. Being a curious bird, the chickadee is often the first bird to appear at a new feeder, exploring the new environment and its safety. In the winter months, the chickadee will join flocks consisting of many other bird species, like warblers, woodpeckers, and nuthatches. These flocks depend on the chickadee to alert the group to a good food source that they can all enjoy. Chickadee medicine involves a strong loyalty to a diverse community.

If chickadee has flown your way as a totem, it is time to explore your world, your dreams, and yourself, without hesitation. If this little chickadee can take on a predator, so can you take on your most stubborn inhibitions and move through the world undaunted by its real or apparent dangers. Be willing to express your truth at all times, and remind the others in your flock to do the same.

### Connecting with Chickadee Medicine

Being bold like the chickadee means meeting your fears head on. Make a list of everything that your fears prevent you from doing. Take on the power of chickadee and find a way to do everything on your list, even in small ways. Chickadee also carries the energy of exploration. It may be time to be a little adventurous and explore places you have never been, even in your own neighborhood. Eat at new restaurants or shop at new stores to connect with the curiosity of chickadee. Don't forget to share what you find on your travels as the chickadee alerts his or her flock to new food sources.

# Finch

*medicine:* power of song and voice, new opportunities

*family:* Fringillidae

*diet:* seeds, insects

*habitat:* pine and laurel forests, sand dunes, orchards, parks, and gardens

The finch family includes some of the most loved songbirds on the planet. Canaries, goldfinches, pine siskins, and many other favorites fit into this large family. They are generally cheerful, musical, and social birds, and delightful to both watch and listen to. These birds are signals of a high level of energy coming into your life, and bring the hope of excitement and joy. Native Americans view the finch as an oracle of celebration and upcoming festivities because of their spontaneous natures and the brilliantly colored plumage of many of the different bird species.

The finch family is diverse, expressing a need for variety in life. If a finch totem enters your life, you are being asked to find new ways to achieve success, joy, and contentment. Your perspective may be too limited at present, causing you to miss opportunities in other directions. The canary, a favorite member of the finch family, is extremely sensitive to its surrounding atmosphere. They will quickly die when noxious gases or other strong toxins are in the near vicinity. Coal miners used to take caged canaries into the mines to detect dangerous gas levels in the tunnels. Those with canary medicine are likewise sensitive to the energies around them, and will become agitated when exposed to negativity or impurities.

## *Connecting with Finch Medicine*

The finch is a very diverse species, inhabiting much of the planet. Those with finch medicine should explore the many different cultures of earth, and travel if finances permit. Enjoying a rich and varied social life is another excellent way to connect with the energy of the finch family. Try new and exciting activities that have previously been out of your normal boundaries, and relish the new experiences and people to be found there. Color therapy also works well for those with a finch totem. Surround yourself with flowers, or wear brightly colored clothing. Both of these are natural energy boosters and will give you a deep understanding of the spirit of finch wisdom.

# Wren

*medicine:* humility, cunning, activity

*family:* Troglodytidae

*diet:* insects

*habitat:* sparsely wooded country, to rain forest areas

The wren has been called "the king of the birds" for centuries. The reason for this exalted title comes from an old myth about how the wren outsmarted the eagle to claim lordship over all of the winged ones. The Gaelic version describes how all of the birds gathered together, for one time only, to determine who would be called the king of all the birds. They decided to have a flying contest, and the bird that flew the highest would win the exalted title. The eagle, of course, flew to the greatest height, and claimed three times that he was the king. The wren, however, being small and cunning, had hidden himself within the down of the eagle, and at that moment flew out and above the eagle. The wren was then given the title of "king of the birds," and has remained an admired bird since.

This story carries a very strong message for those with a wren totem. Just as the small bird could only reach the highest places with the aid of the eagle, we, as students of the universe, must sometimes rely on the wisdom and strength of others to achieve our most lofty ideals and spiritual progress. It may be time to seek out someone wiser than yourself before you proceed so that you too may fly to the heights. Wren medicine is about using your resources to achieve your goals, and sometimes this means looking outside of ourselves.

The wren symbolizes wisdom and divinity in many ancient cultures, and was revered by the Celts as the most sacred of birds. It was called the *Drui-en,* or druid bird, and was the bird of oracular usage among the druids themselves. The Welsh word *Dryw* means both druid and wren, signaling a very ancient connection between the two. In Celtic tradition the druid was seen as a cunning man, able to go through the world under a cloak of invisibility just as the wren in the old folktale did. A wren totem will aid in the silent progress toward success and accomplishment.

The wren is resourceful and bold. As a totem, it advises us to make progress each day in our lives and strive for continual movement. It is an active little bird and a master at migration. These attributes of the wren bring forth the ability to remain grounded during life's constant shifts and changes.

### Connecting with Wren Medicine

The wren can teach you how to use your wits to make the most of your environment. The story of the wren and the eagle demonstrates that using our heads rather than our physical power can be the best path to attainment. The wren is cunning, and as a totem guide will show you the prowess of the mind and the possibilities to outsmart those around if such a situation should arise. Use your resources and become the master of your destiny like the little wren.

# Lark

*medicine:* the mystery of sound, sacred song

*family:* Alaudidae

*diet:* insects and seeds

*habitat:* open country, often nests on ground

The lark is a small to medium passerine bird that has become famous in world mythology and literature for its elaborate singing. Shakespeare once wrote "Hark! Hark! The lark at heaven's gate sings," paying tribute to the extravagant and melodious songs of this little bird. They are dramatic in their display flights, making these birds masters of sound and show. In medieval times, the lark was believed to sing at the gates of Heaven. It has long been considered a bird of poets, along with the nightingale and the thrush, and many have called it the "herald of the dawn" and the center of eternity.

To the ancient alchemists, the lark was thought of as a symbol of sublimation. Sublimation refers to the act of directing energy from its immediate goal to one of a higher order, or to make something purer and more noble. It teaches the power of song to express our inner joy and purpose, and to connect us to our primal life source. If the lark comes your way, you will be surrounded with the mysteries of music, sound, and the power of the voice. The shamanic aspects of sacred song will become predominant in your life as you learn the secrets and science of harmony.

Some Native American tribes believe that the appearance of a lark heralds a time of inner journeying, but it will be a joyful exploration rather than the challenging quests brought by birds like eagle and owl. The lark signals a time of understanding who you are and of finding your own sacred song that expresses your true self to the core. The lark will bring increased intuition and a sense of harmony and acceptance of yourself and your world.

### Connecting with Lark Medicine

Have you ever heard a piece of music that seemed in total harmony with your life? My life, for example, seems to dance to the works of Vivaldi, or Chopin, or Bach. Some pieces appear to capture the very essence of who I am and what I feel. This is the power of music—to reflect our essential spiritual natures on the earth. Likewise, using our voices to *sing* about our lives can have a very profound effect on the ways in which we carry them out. Notice the connections between music and your life—then find ways to join them together meaningfully.

# Waxwing

*medicine:* embracing change, identity, illusion

*family:* Bombycillidae

*diet:* fruit

*habitat:* woodlands, farms, orchards

Waxwings are beautiful birds, characterized by soft, silky plumage. They have "masked" faces, adding a mysterious allure to their appearance and making them totems of identity and illusion. I had the fortunate experience of watching an entire flock of cedar waxwings when they discovered the berry bushes that surround my Alberta home. Their appearance is stunning—they look like paintings that have come to life. When a waxwing totem appears to you, it is time to solidify your identity in the world. You must examine what mask you wear and present to the world, and determine if it is what you really believe yourself to be.

Waxwings are fanatics for fruit, and will delay mating until their favorite fruits are plentiful. Part of their mating ritual, in fact, involves passing fruit back and forth as a gesture of affection. Symbolically, these behaviors reflect an inherent love of the sweetest things in life, and will reveal much about the preferences of the person with the waxwing totem.

Waxwing also teaches us how to use ceremonial masks to connect with spiritual energies and powers. Masks serve as transformation devices, and are used by shamans all over the world in order that they may temporarily become another being. It may be a time to undertake some of these ancient ritual practices in order to expand your present state of awareness. Transformation is crucial to the process of self-realization, and the waxwing helps us slide from one mask to another while maintaining a solid sense of our foundation on earth.

## Connecting with Waxwing Medicine

The waxwing is a master of persona. This fantastic bird will teach you the power of personal identity, and the various masks we wear for different people. To connect with the waxwing's wisdom, create different kinds of ceremonial masks for yourself. Imagine your entire persona transforming with each new mask you wear and become aware of its power to change a part of your inner being as well. This exercise will allow you to see the temporary nature of the physical persona, and the often-illusory impressions we have of ourselves and others.

## Mockingbird

*medicine:* reflection, voice, being heard rather than seen

*family:* Mimidae

*diet:* insects, berries, seeds

*habitat:* country, farmland

The mockingbird was given its name because of its imitation of the sounds it hears. This bird will mimic the cries of other birds, and even car alarms, as long as the sounds are short and repetitive. Mockingbirds will sing the loudest during the twilight hours when the sun is on the horizon. They, too, seem to greet the dawn like other songbirds, making them heralds of morning. Northern mockingbirds have been known to sing during the full moon giving them a profound connection to nature's rhythms and cycles.

Aggressive birds, mockingbirds are known to harass and attack domestic pets, like a cat or dog, and sometimes humans as well when they feel they are being threatened. Mockingbird as a spirit guide can teach us how to keep out of our lives the people who threaten our well-being and sense of comfort. We must all be aggressive at times in order to maintain the boundaries of our own personal space.

Mockingbird teaches a valuable lesson about mimicry. What we mimic in our lives will be reflected back to us in our experiences, which allows us to see what we truly are or what we are striving to become. This is a hard lesson to learn at times, for we often see that we are imitating those things or beings that are contrary to our true natures and desires. Another lesson of mockingbird is that of voice, and what we are saying to the world. Mockingbird, being a very plain bird in appearance, has a powerful voice. Those with a mockingbird totem will not be flashy on the outside, like the peacock or the parrot, but will carry their strength in the messages they send out with their words.

### Connecting with Mockingbird Medicine

Your voice is a powerful tool for manifestation. The mockingbird can show you how to use your voice to affect your reality. The things we say will reverberate throughout the universe and come back to us as a tangible experience. When we learn this, we are better equipped to take control of our lives. Work with the mockingbird to enhance your understanding of this most ancient law. Practicing the recitation of mantras or affirmations will strengthen the power of your voice and make it a more effective tool in your spiritual progress.

## Thrush

*medicine:* love, poetry, song

*family:* Turdidae

*habitat:* wooded areas

*diet:* insectivorous, will also eat worms, snails, and fruit

This elusive bird is small like a sparrow, and prefers high altitudes. Members of the thrush family, particularly the Bicknell's thrush, gravitate to mountainous areas, enjoying the cool damp climate. They are hard to find and are considered secretive in their habits. The bluebird and robin are members of the thrush family, as is the common blackbird. A study of these birds will serve to enhance the meaning of the entire thrush family.

The thrush is considered the bird of devotion, fertility, peace, abundance, and youth. It is the totem of writers, singers, poets, and songwriters—a connection that goes back to when the Greek poet Homer was given a caged thrush after reciting a beautiful poem. The thrush helps us remember the ancient language of love, trust, and empathy. Its medicine teaches us how to cast out fears that prevent the opening of our hearts to others.

### Connecting with Thrush Medicine

As another bird connected to the literary arts, writing songs and poetry will allow you to capture its essence as a totem. Its wisdom encourages a deep healing of the heart, allowing the receptivity of love into your life. Meditating on the heart chakra is a wonderful way to connect with this bird. Allow your heart center to open and be receptive to love and abundance in its many forms.

## Robin

*medicine:* growth, new beginnings, fertility

*family:* Turdidae

*diet:* invertebrates, fruits, berries

*habitat:* woodland, open farmland, urban areas

Robins are a welcome sight to many after a long, cold winter. They appear as the herald of the springtime, scampering across our front lawns in search of the goodies that accompany the thaw. The American robin is a migratory songbird belonging to the thrush family. It is mostly active during the day, and congregates in large flocks at night. The male robin has a complex and beautiful song, and its characteristic running and stopping across the front lawn make this bird species very distinguishable. It was a sacred bird to the pagans of Ireland and England, and old legends say that faeries were fearful of robins and could not shape shift into this bird form. It was called the storm-cloud bird in Norse mythology, and was considered sacred to the god Thor. Robin was a culture hero among the Tlingit peoples of North America, created by raven to please people with its song. It is revered in most cultures as a fun-loving and fortuitous bird, and is a classic symbol of the return of the spring.

The robin as a totem teaches the ability to accept new life. This is difficult for many as it involves letting go of the old as a preliminary step. When you are aligned with the robin's power, you will ease through life's transitions with greater fluidity and acceptance, allowing the springtime of *your* life to enter in full bloom. It is a powerful symbol of the spring equinox and the sacred powers of this seasonal celebration. If a robin has come to you as a totem, it is time to move forward and live a new life. There are things that must be cast aside for new growth to occur. As a harbinger of change, the robin will endow you with the strength to embrace the light of a new day with joy and peace in your heart.

### Connecting with Robin Medicine

Robin is the herald of the springtime and the renewal of life after the long winter season. If you are working with the robin, it is essential that you work closely with plants and flowers during the spring and summer months. Connecting with this bird means connecting with the energies of the earth's renewal. Watching the world in bloom anew will bring you closer to the message of robin concerning the natural cycles of death and new life. If you are comfortable and knowledgable with ritual magic, conduct a ritual on the spring equinox, celebrating the arrival of spring. This celebration should include a symbolic "giving away" of things that do not fit the new life you are calling forth with the dawning of this cycle.

## Bluebird

*medicine:* happiness, gentleness, contentment

*family:* Turdidae

*diet:* insects

*habitat:* open country

If you have ever seen a mountain bluebird, you can attest to how striking its color is. I once had a little bluebird fly in front of my car, and the flash was so bright it took me a minute to figure out what it was. A member of the thrush family, the bluebird is a long-cherished symbol of happiness and contentment. This little bird reminds us not to get so wrapped up in everyday living that we forget to take time for our own pleasure and well-being. It is a symbol of cheerfulness, joy, the hearth and home, and new births.

The bluebird has a long mythology around the world and is held as a sacred bird in many cultures. The Navajo sing a *Bluebird Song* to remind everyone in the tribe to wake at dawn and greet the sun. The mythology from another Native American tribe recounts how bluebird was the first-born son of the sun. In magical symbolism, bluebirds are used to represent the positive aspects of confidence and the negative aspects of egotism. Because of their predominantly blue coloring, these birds have strong connections to sky energies. Their feathers have been used to call in the rains, and are sometimes thought to be symbolic of snow and ice as well.

Those with a bluebird totem exude gentleness and peace-fulness. They will only assert themselves when threatened, and are content and joyful in the simplest things in life. Bluebird medicine teaches us how to walk in peace, and the teachings of this little bird are reminiscent of the stillness and tranquility of sunrise. It is a great blessing to receive bluebird medicine and should be taken with great care and respect.

## *Connecting with Bluebird Medicine*

The bluebird is one of the most peaceful of birds, and carries a powerful message for those whom it chooses to guide. To connect with this bird, you must learn how to live your life from a place of inner calm and joy. I believe that many people trained in the Buddhist tradition carry bluebird medicine. Free of the concerns of the ego, this little bird teaches you to walk in the ways of peace. Try studying ancient meditation techniques to connect with bluebird, and free yourself from the concerns of the world.

## Blackbird

*medicine:* enchantment, inner call

*families:* Turdidae, Icteridae

*diet:* omnivorous—insects, earthworms, berries, seeds

*habitat:* woodland areas, prefers dense undergrowth

The blackbird has deep and ancient connections to the powers of song. It was known as Rhiannon's bird, revered in Celtic lore as the gatekeeper to the otherworld and the realm of the faeries. It was once said that when the blackbirds were in the otherworld they would shed their black feathers and become "rainbow birds." They are birds of mysticism, magic, and enchantment, and signal a time of deeper understanding of the powers of nature within our lives.

The hypnotic song of the blackbird is said to lull the waking mind, and consequently awaken the psychic mind. He invites us to enter and explore the mysteries and follow a deeper, more spiritual path that will expand our consciousness and perceptive knowing. People with blackbird medicine often have within themselves the ability to heal others with sound.

The red-winged blackbird, my personal favorite, has a special symbolic meaning because of the black, red, and yellow coloring of its plumage. Ted Andrews explains how this bird has ties to the level Binah on the Qubalistic Tree of Life.[24] This level is associated with the Dark Mother, and thus to the primal feminine energies of nature.

---

24. *Animal Speak*, Llewellyn, 1993

The blackbird carries the wisdom of the life force and the primal powers of the earth. Look for these ancient energies manifesting in your life and allow the influx of mystical energies to flow around you. With a blackbird totem you will experience the enchantment of the natural world—a world that is always magical, beautiful, and eternally alive.

### Connecting with Blackbird Medicine

Attracting blackbirds to your yard will help you understand their very ancient mysticism. The red-winged blackbird, in particular, is soothing and mysterious in song, and will open your eyes to the world of natural magic. The one thing you will notice about the blackbird's song is the eerie way it echoes into the distance as if penetrating the veil of our reality. You will always know when one of these birds is visiting your yard. Use your own voice for channeling the mystical energies of song. This is also a great way of tapping into your inner being that lies below the surface of your waking mind.

## Starling

*medicine:* adaptability

*family:* Sturnidae

*diet:* insects

*habitat:* urban and suburban areas, farmland, playing fields, golf courses

The starling embodies the importance of quick adaptation to new environments, and the need to develop new skills and acclimatize to different ways of life. It is considered the totem of migrants, drifters, tourists, and those who move often for work purposes. Starling people are quick to learn new customs and languages, and the traditional ways of different cultures. It is in their nature to adapt. The starling is another community-oriented bird, keeping its strength in numbers. If a larger bird attempts an attack, the entire flock will attack the bird to drive it off. Despite its small size, the starling is proud and confident, knowing he can depend on his flock to help if trouble arises. It is often the totem of those who fight for good causes and who defend the whole group when challenged.

The starling prefers to live in urban areas where there are abundant resources for feeding and nesting. This reflects its ability to fit in wherever it goes, and it can tolerate large populations. The starling has an interesting courting process, and will use decorations, such as flowers or green material in order to attract a mate. This reflects the tendency of starling people to make a home out of any environment. Starling is sociable, loves being in large groups, and can be forceful when the need arises.

People with a starling totem can be found wherever there are social dynamics at play. Striving to fit in with the crowd and be a part of the bustling community are top priorities for starling people. If the starling appears to you as a teacher, you are to learn the ways of social adaptation. This bird often appears during times of transition to aid in the process of adjustment that follows.

## *Connecting with Starling Medicine*

Starling carries the wisdom of adapting to any situation that comes your way. You will enhance your connection to this bird by socializing in different environments with new and interesting people. Like the finch species, starlings are capable of living and thriving just about anywhere. In nature, this is an extremely important skill, and in the modern world of global communication, it is certainly an asset to anyone. Making improvements to your home by adding comforts and personal touches will increase the social energy in your home and promote greater activity and unity. Spend time socializing in your home to connect with the starling's sense of social cohesiveness.

# Swallow/Martin

*medicine:* perspective, objectivity

*family:* Hirundinidae

*diet:* insects

*habitat:* grassland, open woodland, marshes, savanna, mangroves, scrub land

The swallow is one of the heralds of the summer season and seems to follow warm weather everywhere. It was one of the sacred birds of Isis, the Egyptian Mother Goddess, as well as Aphrodite and her Roman counterpart, Venus. In Rome it was believed that the swallow represented the young innocent souls of those who died at birth. The swallow is considered in many legends to have brought fire from the heavens. In Native American folklore, the swallow carried fire from the sun on her tail feathers, which is why they are colored red.

In ancient Egypt, during the Old Kingdom, the swallow (*menet*) was symbolic of the stars, and as such the imperishable souls of the dead. Swallows rode in the prow of Ra's boat. In Spell 1216 of the *Pyramid Texts*, the Pharaoh describes how he has "gone to the great island in the midst of the Field of Offerings on which the swallow gods alight; the swallows are the imperishable stars." In the *Book of the Dead*, chapter 86 instructs the dead on how to transform into a swallow. In Medieval times it was believed that the swallow knew of a magical stone or a magical herb that could restore eyesight.

Swallows are accomplished, graceful fliers that are able to maneuver the sky with great precision and speed. They are aerial acrobats, flying and swooping after insects all over North and South America. They are able to change direction during flight in order to pursue their meals, a feat only possible because of their streamlined bodies. The purple martin, measuring up to twenty centimeters, is the largest member of the swallow family. The coloring of this species also points to the mystical qualities of this bird and its ability to move swiftly through many different realms. People with this totem, like the crow and raven totems, will have excellent maneuverability between worlds and states of consciousness. If the swallow has come as your totem, you will need to traverse your current path with great care, swiftness, and accuracy. The messages of this bird totem are that of perspective and swift action. You are being asked to look at your chosen path from multiple angles before moving ahead.

## *Connecting with Swallow/Martin Medicine*

There are several great meditation exercises that will give you a better perspective of the swallows and martins. Imagine yourself trying to reach a goal that is blocked by some kind of obstacle. For each one, create several ways in order to overcome the obstacle. This gives your mind greater flexibility that will manifest in your ability to move through real obstacles that may hinder your path. The swallow teaches us great navigational skills along our path, but we must be willing to look at alternate routes to achieve our desired goals.

Birds of
Shining Color

This section includes some of the most visually spectacular birds on the planet. Contained within the wisdom of all of these birds is the earth's natural expression of joy through the beauty of light and the colors thereupon produced. As you will see, colorful birds have always held a special place in the human psyche.

## Hummingbird

*medicine:* shaman's messenger, joy, beauty, love

*family:* Trochilidae

*diet:* nectar

*habitat:* any natural setting with adequate food supply: meadows, urban areas, farmland, coastal areas

The hummingbird is one of nature's smallest miracles, but holds a large and ancient spiritual history. An Andean mystic once said of the tiny bird: "When we watch the hummingbird, the living symbol of ….the sun, we embrace the joy of spirit."[25]

I have watched many hummingbirds dance outside my window, sometimes alone, other times in pairs, but always whirring about with an almost otherworldly source of energy. Perhaps it is the energy of pure spirit that gives them such speed, or the instinctual drive to enjoy all that it can while on earth. Hummingbirds are messengers too, waking up our sense of joy and unbounded wonder at the world.

The hummingbird can hover in midair, flapping its small wings up to ninety times per second. The birds' name actually

---

25. Americo Yabar, Andean mystic and Paqo

comes from the humming sound of their wings when in this frenzied state of flight. They are important pollinators, feeding on nectar with only the strongest sugar content, and they serve much the same function as bees in the spreading of pollen to produce more flowers. They are the spreaders of new life in the bird kingdom, and manifest the fullest expression of joy by creating new life.

Hummingbirds have the highest metabolism of all animals, and those close to their medicine are fairly easy to recognize. Hummingbird people are always doing *something*, and thrive on the energy that everyday life provides. They walk and talk a little faster, get more done than most of us, and are generally happier people to be around. This sense of frenzy comes from the hummingbird's short life span, as many of them don't even survive their first year. People with this totem will always live in the present and see life as too short to harbor fear, worry, or anger about anything. They are lively individuals with much natural enthusiasm.

Hummingbird wisdom personifies following your bliss. It is an adventure of the senses when this little bird flies into your life. You can expect great energy, whether creative, emotional, physical, or spiritual, for this is a bird of the higher realms. To the indigenous Andean peoples, hummingbird is symbolic of the Upper World, the realm of refined creative energy. It is from this dimension that the hummingbird brings messages to the *Paqo* shaman. The Mayans also believed that the hummingbird was connected to the fifth world.

Hummingbird's ability to fly in all directions is truly extraordinary. This bird can traverse all places in the universe, from the stars to the earth, and imparts this spiritual gift to those the hummingbird chooses to teach. If hummingbird has come to your side as a teacher, you must treat this winged being with much respect. Hummingbird disdains ugliness and harshness, and will not linger long in such an energy field.

Many believe that hummingbird is the creature that opens the heart. Hummingbird consciousness awakens refinement of taste and a heightened expression of, and appreciation for, beauty in all its forms. Because of their magical qualities, hummingbird feathers have been used for a millennium in the making of love charms; hummingbird awakens love as no other animal can.

Those working with this wisdom will have abundant energy, and will seem to radiate joy and gratitude. Shamans who have hummingbird allies may appear almost delirious when attuned with hummingbird consciousness. This is a fragile medicine, and maintaining a positive energy balance is a particular challenge for the hummingbird due to its highly energetic lifestyle. At night, hummingbirds enter a coma-like state, known as torpor, which is accompanied by a lowering of body temperature. This enables the hummingbird to sustain itself through the night while it is inactive and not producing body heat through its characteristic energetic flight. Those attuned with hummingbird consciousness tend to have extremes in physical energy. They will be magnetic individuals with very social lives.

Hummingbird will often appear to those who have forgotten how to enjoy simple beauty in life, and is a call to witness the joy of creation once more. In South American religion, the hummingbird was the symbol for resurrection, due to its continual return every spring. The Pueblo Indians have hummingbird dances and use their feathers in rituals to bring rain, and Pueblo shamans use hummingbirds as couriers to deliver gifts to the Great Mother Goddess, who dwells beneath the earth.

Hummingbirds aid shamans in keeping the world in balance. As seekers of beauty and harmony, these feathered beings impart the ability to enjoy nature.

In the Aztec religion the most powerful of the gods was Huitzilopochtli, whose name is derived from a compound word *huitzilin*, meaning "hummingbird" and "sorcerer that spits fire." Huitzilopochtli was himself depicted as wearing the head of a hummingbird as a helmet, and Aztec royalty and priests often wore capes adorned with hummingbird feathers. Because hummingbirds have a fierce territoriality, Aztec warriors were believed to reincarnate as these birds, and the Aztecs would decorate the cloaks of kings entirely of hummingbird skins.

### Connecting with Hummingbird Medicine

The hummingbird dances through the world at a magnificent speed. If you want to be like hummingbird, find new ways of increasing your body's natural energy. Things that will help this process include walking outdoors daily; eating lots of fruits, vegetables, and other organic foods; and avoiding processed foods. If you enjoy sweet things as the hummingbird does, try switching to honey or natural cane sugar. Walk among the flowers each day and delight in the natural beauty of the world around you. This helps to stimulate gratitude and joy, which overflows with a hummingbird totem. Plant a garden, if you do not already have one overflowing with flowers. Being close to flowers will enhance your understanding of the hummingbird's natural love of these beautiful expressions of nature. There really is nothing complicated about connecting to this wonderful bird. It is the simplest enjoyment of life and all the earth has to offer.

## Peacock

*medicine:* pride, beauty, past-life connections

*family:* Pavoninidae

*diet:* ticks, termites, ants, mice, locusts, plants, flower petals, seed heads, scorpions, reptiles

*habitat:* open forest, bushland, thorn forest, rain forest

A visually stunning bird, the peacock holds a special place in world mythology. Only the male of this species is called a peacock—the female is called a peahen. Long held as the national bird of India, ancient kings were said to have peacock gardens where guests could enjoy the spectacular peacock mating dance—a tradition dating back many centuries. Ancient Babylon had a Peacock Throne, and the birds were symbols of royalty there and in Persia. The peacock symbolizes the power and beauty of transmutation. It is said to have the ability to eat poisons and transform them into the beauty of its feathers.

The tail feathers of this bird have no doubt given rise to the peacock's exalted position around the world. They have been valued for centuries for their iridescent blue and green hues, and the mysterious symbolism of the "eyes" continues to this day. Peacock as a totem has come to mean karmic connections and past-life memories. When the bird appears to you as a teacher, you will be experiencing nostalgia for long-lost incarnations, or will be required to resolve a past-life karmic debt.

The peacock has been considered a sacred bird since medieval times where the most solemn oaths were taken "on the peacock." It is also the closest in physical description to the legendary phoenix, who rises from its own ashes after being consumed in the flames of destruction. Thus, it has remained a bird of rebirth and resurrection to this day.

The peacock has often been called the guardian of the gates of paradise, and represents the riches of body, mind, and soul. It symbolizes royalty, divinity, power, beauty, and vanity. While impressing a future mate, the peacock is undoubtedly sure of his success and proud of his grand display. A polygamous bird, the peacock enjoys courtship.

The peacock as a totem shares the wisdom of self-esteem. This is not to be confused with ego pride, but rather the recognition of self-worth as a divine being. The human race suffered a devastating blow with the Christian notion of natural sin. This view is nihilistic and leaves no room for true self love and respect. Peacock summons you to "walk your talk" and share your gifts and inner beauty with the world in a peaceful and joyful way.

Peacock medicine also explores past lives, and considers how our former incarnations are affecting us now. The eyes of the peacock's tail are said to be able to view time as a single event, allowing the soul's progress to be uninterrupted by the concepts of past, present, and future. If peacock arrives, you will be seeing many things, or feeling many emotions that are coming forth from past-life memories. Oftentimes, the peacock shares this wisdom when there are unresolved issues that are rearing their heads in our present incarnations. This can be painful, bringing forth feelings of great nostalgia, fear, or sadness, but they are as much a part of who we are as our experiences in this lifetime.

### Connecting with Peacock Medicine

Meditation techniques specifically geared toward past life recall will aid you in your connection to peacock's wisdom. You may also look for clues in dreams, or in daily events that trigger memories relating to a different incarnation. Try meditating on the peacock's tail feather. Look at the image of the eye and imagine it as being a portal into the past where we can access the most distant of memories. You may also need to work on self-esteem issues. Try wearing more colorful clothing that mirrors the glorious colors in the peacock's feathers. Finally, stand tall. The peacock is a proud bird, accepting its beauty without hesitation, and has an obvious sense of its own importance in the world—you should too!

## Parrot

*medicine:* communication between human and animal, color healing

*family:* Psittaciformes

*diet:* seeds, fruit, nectar, pollen, insects

*habitat:* tropical and subtropical forests

A magnificent species of bird, parrots give the medicine of color to the world, and the healing everyone experiences through its beauty. People who carry parrot medicine are often drawn to the visual arts, even costume design, or wherever they can work with colors on a daily basis. Color is the greatest healer for those with this bird totem, and they will often incorporate bright colors in their clothing and home furnishings.

The most famous and accomplished human voice mimics are found among parrots. The parrot's ability to speak human language has made it a link between the human and animal world for centuries. Parrot teaches us how to bridge the illusory gap between the two kingdoms, and work together to help our planet as one united group. Parrots are loud and often defiant birds. They engage in loud chatter, squeaks, piping, trills, rattles, and yelps. Several parrot species even engage in duets, with two or more, birds taking part in a single prolonged vocalization. This is believed to function primarily as a way to strengthen a pair bond. The power of voice is an important part of parrot's teachings, and if chosen by this bird you will come to a deep understanding of the impact of your words on your present reality. Our voice carries vibrations that aid in the manifestation of experience. What we say will have a ripple effect, causing either positive manifestations, or negative repercussions.

Parrots have very long life spans, and have been known to outlive their human companions. This longevity is revered in primitive groups where survival is more precarious and uncertain. They are sociable and affectionate birds, traits that will be reflected in the parrot totem individual.

In India, the god of love, Kama, rode on a parrot as his preferred vehicle. One of his sacred birds was the parrot as a symbol of his physical beauty. In ancient Rome, the parrot held the post of herald of the emperors, announcing their arrival to the Roman citizens.

Parrot is also a bird of the sun. It is the bringer of news and revealer of secrets in Afro-Caribbean lore. Among the Yanomami people of the Amazonian basin, parrot feathers are particularly prized for their healing and protective properties. The feathers are often attached to arrows and sent into the skies, requesting healing from the deities and abundance for the village.

## Connecting with Parrot Medicine

The parrot, being connected with goddesses of love and beauty, speaks to the feminine side of our natures. Give some more attention to your inner goddess (or god) and do something to enhance your appearance. This will give your confidence a boost and allow you to shine a little brighter. Wearing bright colors will also raise the vibration of your entire being and bring you closer to the parrot's wisdom. Color can have a very profound effect on the psyche, often on a subconscious level.

Birds of
the City

City birds are some of the most clever and humorous birds on earth. I include under this heading the crows, ravens, magpies, seagulls, and pigeons for their endless curiosity, adaptability, and willingness to not only live in, but also challenge and manipulate the human world.

One of my most enduring bird memories involved a pair of crows on a utility wire outside of my kitchen window. They were perched beside each other at first, until a squirrel came running along the cable. One of the crows got up and flew to the other side of the squirrel, and then it dawned on me at last that they were teasing the poor critter by not letting it get past them on either side. The crows just sat there, while the squirrel paced back and forth trying to get down. Squirrels and dogs seem to be the favorite targets for the humor of many of these city birds, and my late pooch Kalem suffered much psychological trauma at the expense of hungry and clever magpies.

I have included in this section the great scavengers of the bird world. Although they may also fit into other categories, I felt that the crow, raven, magpie, seagull, and pigeon deserved a place all their own. They are wildly intelligent, and, unlike many other birds, have learned the meaning of the phrase "If you can't beat them, join them." They have adapted to the ridiculous population growths, pollution, and technology of our modern world, and will take advantage of it in every conceivable way. If one of these birds is a spirit companion of yours you will no doubt share in their versatility, keen wit, and intelligence, and will probably have some tricks of your own for surviving life in the modern world. Here we will honor the rich history of the city birds, whose presence and antics never cease to amaze and delight.

## Crow and Raven

*medicine:* magic, death, prophecy, healing, shape-shifting, universal law

*family:* Corvidae

*diet:* omnivorous

*habitat:* wilderness, farmland, parks, open woodlands, and cities

Perhaps two of the most enigmatic of all the birds, crows and ravens remain a paradox in the modern world. They have proven their intelligence over and over again, and they are also known for their abilities to plan their actions and then carry them out, understand number sequences, and make simple tools. Yet despite their smarts and adaptability, they continue to be persecuted as pests—as creatures capable of making your skin crawl.

Crows and ravens are among the bird entities most frequently mentioned in world mythology, religion, and magic, and known as masters of shape shifting, shamanic travel, and prophecy. In Ireland, the phrase "raven's knowledge" refers to the oracular ability to see and know everything. They are capable of a wide range of vocalizations, and have been famed since antiquity for their ability to mimic human speech.

In Norse mythology, the great god Odin was accompanied by two ravens, Hugin and Munin, meaning "thought" and "memory." Odin, as the chief god of Norse paganism, was associated with wisdom, war, battle, and death, as well as poetry, prophesy, and magic. This gives greater strength to raven's role in magical traditions, and is reminiscent of its associations with the Celtic battle goddess Morrigan. Crows are scavengers, so it is darkly fitting that they should be linked to the carnage wrought by swords and war axes. During the tenth and eleventh centuries CE, Viking chieftains and rulers carried into battle a raven banner that was considered to have been totemic in nature. Scholars believe this raven flag was symbolic of Odin as the "raven-god," and could only be made by the virgin daughters of the Viking hero-warriors.

Ravens have also been long regarded as messengers of the sun in many traditions, and were sacred to King Arthur. Both Arthur and Bran received their "divine king" status from the sun, which reveals the ancient connection between the sun gods and the raven totem. The Greeks, much like the Egyptians, looked to the raven and crow with great affection and good humor. The Greeks, however, also harbored a hidden terror of these magical birds, and viewed them with fear, awe, and nervous laughter. To the Greeks, they represented the realm of nature persisting even in cities— creatures largely beyond the control of either human beings or gods. A Graeco-Egyptian priest from the third century BCE recounted how crows were an important symbolic image in Egypt. They were considered symbols of faithful love, largely due to their monogamous nature. Ravens and crows were thus believed to be the earthly manifestation of the divine idealized love that was usually portrayed by the dove, or some other white bird.

In Siberian mythology, the mythical time of creation is associated with Raven. He was either portrayed as a demiurge or an assistant who carried out the orders of a powerful sky god. Raven has a considerable amount of shamanic power in many cultures, and is sometimes seen as a patriarch or great-grandfather and the primordial ancestor of humans. Raven is the great trickster in mythologies from Polynesia and North America—an attribute that seems to mirror to perfection the essential nature of the raven family. These birds have a rich mythological history in Europe as well, and embody the attributes of death and destruction.

Crows and ravens are adaptable and cunning, and are clever enough to enjoy a joke at someone else's expense. They are unparalleled in wit and street smarts, and their ability to adapt and survive in any environment is a great source of power. This a lesson of great importance for those chosen as students of these birds. We all live many lifetimes, and within each one we undergo continual change and shifts in experience. Crow and raven remind us that we are more adaptable than we think. We embrace change over and over again and make use of our resources the best way we can. In terms of social intelligence, most crows are highly sociable beings, but the raven is a solitary bird, at home in rocky valleys and lonely hills. Although all members of this bird family share many characteristics, the raven is often portrayed as more closely connected to magic and the mysteries—probably due to its solitary and elusive nature.

Working with crow or raven wisdom can be challenging, as the lessons they bring involve death, transmutation, and great change. It is said that crow is the keeper of Universal Law, or the laws of Great Spirit in the Native American tradition. If you carry strong crow or raven medicine, you have a deep understanding of how the universe works and the relationship between its many realms and creatures. Crow and raven are the primordial shape shifters, and have conquered the illusions of time and space. If you are working with the wisdom of either of these birds you can expect to see many different perspectives of the world, as crow and raven see the past, present, and future simultaneously. If a crow or raven totem enters your life, there is some kind of magic at play in your life. Things are moving as if by divine orchestration, and you are right at the center of your own destiny.

The changes that crow and raven bring will be inevitable. Connecting with these birds for spiritual progress will ease the transitions and make the lessons more beneficial to your being. Crows and ravens, although carrying heavy medicines, do enjoy having fun. Do not take the changes *too* seriously or you may miss a big part of the message at hand. Finding many crow or raven feathers is one way these birds may get your attention, and they are commonly found in urban areas. When I began working with crow, I would find between one and three crow feathers *every day*! You can imagine how fast they added up.

Crow and raven bring the Great Mystery to your doorstep. This medicine asks that you understand your part in the cosmos and own all parts of yourself and your experience. They are symbols of the void, the black hole in space, and the timeless transition between all worlds. In the Norse shamanic tradition, ravens symbolize the powers of necromancy, telepathy, and clairvoyance. Being able to merge all time into one reality, crow and raven can impart the prophetic eye unto those who honor them. Boria Sax, in her fascinating book *Crow,* discusses the paradox of crow and raven throughout history: "In the human imagination, crows have always been creatures of extremes. They are playful and solemn, noisy and articulate, sacred and profane." On one side they represent death, destruction, and the shadows of existence, but on the other, they are bringers of transformation and all the colors that shine forth from the blackness of their being. They are magic and prophesy, birth and creation. Thus, these birds are the duality of all existence, encompassing the dark as well as the light. This is one of the most important lessons of the crow and raven— all is one in the timeless void of creation.

## Connecting with Crow and Raven Medicine

Performing any kind of magical ceremony will connect you to the powers of the crow and raven. Raven is tied more strongly to healing rituals, but both birds will aid in releasing rituals or magic work for bringing an end to some outworn aspect of your life. They carry heavy medicine, and should be approached cautiously as guides, for they are also renowned for their trickster antics. Crow is considered the keeper of the universal laws. You must understand how these laws work in your own life, and how they can be manipulated and utilized by your own inner creator. You will also want to study the ancient art of shape shifting. Both of these birds are heavily connected to transformative powers, such as those used in shamanic work.

## Magpie

*medicine:* occult wisdom, cleverness, boldness

*family:* Corvidae

*diet:* omnivorous

*habitat:* urban areas, wooded areas

The magpie is one of those birds you either love or you hate. They are among the most mischievous and misunderstood birds in the world, but seem to thrive when a good dose of humor is in order. There really is nothing funnier than a magpie teasing a dog in order to cleverly sneak away with its food. They are among nature's finest comedians, and alert the world to their boisterous presence through the raucousness of their voices. They are masters of chatter, and I always enjoy sitting under a tree housing a large group of magpies and listening to their gossip. It is both fascinating and refreshing, and a highly recommended pastime.

Notorious for being thieves attracted to shiny objects, magpies are among the most comical and bold creatures of the avian world. They are hoarders, and will steal what they can to store in their nests for who knows what reason. They will use the same nest year after year, which will become messier as time goes by and it is filled with the stuff Magpie finds from the world around it. These birds generally seem to have a fascination with the world, and love a good laugh at the expense of everyone else.

Magpie is called the "cunning prophet," connecting us to the powers of magic, divination, and otherworldly journeying. The magpie has long been a bird of magic, and has been used for centuries to represent occult powers and wisdom. In Sweden it is believed that sorcerers take the form of magpies on *Walpurgis Night* (a celebration deriving from early pagan spring customs). In the rest of Scandinavia, witches are thought to take this bird form or use them as a means of transport. The Mongolians believed that the magpie was in charge of the weather, and it has been connected to many elements of weather around the world. The tail feathers of the magpie are said to invoke the powers of thunder, and are also believed to be connected to rainbows (and consequently rain) because of their stunning iridescent colors.

The magpie has also gained a bad reputation over the centuries, partly due to its thieving nature, and partly because of its association with witchcraft. The "Christianizing" of many old pagan traditions and animal symbols probably contributed to the magpie's downfall, as well as the biblical story of the Ark. In this story, the magpie was said to be the only animal refusing to enter the boat and instead sat on the roof chattering all day long.

The magpie is known for its bold endeavors, and those with a magpie totem will likely be risk takers in some area of their lives. Magpies tease other animals, often bigger than themselves, in order to win a higher status within their group or to attract a mate. Magpie medicine involves being bold in order to advance ourselves in the world and to achieve our goals. The person with a magpie totem will undoubtedly be very interesting. They may, of course, also appear somewhat obnoxious to others, but they have nothing but lightheartedness in mind. If a magpie appears as a totem, it may be time to lighten up a bit and have some fun of your own. Magpie may also be asking you to accept your innate occult abilities and express yourself through ritual practices. The magpie was one of my first bird totems to appear, and is a very interesting spirit guide. You will be given unique opportunities to experience the spirit world with this bird at your side. Just go with the magpie totem's whims and you will progress in the ways of this wonderful wisdom.

## Connecting with Magpie Medicine

The magpie is principally a bird of the occult practices, so exploration of these areas would benefit your connection to this bird. Use common sense when undertaking any ritual work, however, as magpie is also a great prankster like his crow and raven cousins, and may lead you astray if you are not paying attention. Remember, first and foremost, that the magpie has a tremendous sense of playfulness. You are reminded during your spiritual work not to take it too seriously. It is, after all, only one part of our natures. If you are close to the magpie in spirit, you may need to lighten up, but chances are that you will already have a well-developed sense of humor with this bird hanging around.

# Blue Jay

*medicine:* proper use of personal power

*family:* Corvidae

*diet:* acorns, weed seeds, grain, fruits, peanuts, bread, meat, small invertebrates

*habitat:* pine woods, spruce-fir forests, mixed woodlands, parks, residential areas

The word *Jay* has an interesting background, and actually comes to us from the Latin word *gaia* or *gaea,* which translates to *Mother Earth.* The blue jay's coloring is also closely connected with the elements of earth, sky, and spirit, which are represented by the black, blue, and white, respectively. The sky, symbolized by the blue of the jay's plumage, separates the earth (black) from the heavens (white), making the blue jay a link between all three domains.

Most blue jays have much in common with their crow and magpie cousins. They are very curious and intelligent birds, watching the actions of humans to take advantage of food supplies. Young blue jays enjoy the classic *Corvidae* habit of taking off with shiny objects for fun—and then dropping them when they lose interest. Like their cousins, blue jays are great opportunists, and have adapted remarkably well to the ever-changing world around them. They are excellent mimics, and will often impersonate hawks and other birds in nature. They have also been able to mimic other sounds when captive, such as some human speech and domestic pets, like cats. This is a great trick, and is a part of the blue jay's natural love of play. It may, however, serve as a survival tactic for the blue jay family, scaring away other birds and animals by making them think there is a hawk present. It is a fearless bird and will defend its territorial boundaries with a world-famous aggression.

The Chinook people of the Pacific Coast revere blue jay as a creator god. This deity decides how each animal will live, make its home, and eat. He is also a protector of humans. In the myths surrounding blue jay, he is a braggart, schemer, and mischief-maker in the highest degree. He is the clown of the gods, and when not causing trouble for someone else, is often in trouble himself. This myth no doubt arose from the nature of the blue jay as a trickster and a mimic in the wild.

The medicine of the blue jay involves the proper use of personal power. The power we gain through spiritual growth must be used with responsibility and integrity, and never for the purpose of harming or manipulating others. While we must all accept our unique gifts as inherent sources of power and expression, we must do so only with the intention of the higher good. When the blue jay comes as a totem, most of its hosts have already been exploring many different avenues. The appearance of blue jay is a signal to carry out your potential to its fullest capacity. This bird's crest reminds us that we only achieve mastery through dedication to our path; this "crown" is only given when we operate from the Higher Mind. Blue jay people tend to dabble in many different areas, scattering their energies in too many directions. If you have been visited by blue jay, it is time to become the master of one area of your life and direct your energies fully to the path you choose, carrying it out to its perfection. People with a blue jay totem are naturally inquisitive, which is why it is important not to jump from one thing to another without a firm grasp and mastery first.

Blue jay's power comes from exploring the diversity of the world. His medicine brings an openness to doing things in new and more interesting ways. This bird will actively seek out opportunities and go after that which he desires with a seemingly nonexistent level of fear. If you are seeing a lot of blue jay, it is time to create a solid foundation for yourself by applying your personal power in meaningful ways. You are probably already aware of the direction you are being asked to move, and are reminded that deciding on a path is the first step in achieving your goals. Take on the boldness of the jay and explore your chosen path to the fullest. This is the power of blue jay.

### Connecting with Blue Jay Medicine

Connecting with the power of blue jay means becoming the master of your energies. Work on completing one level of achievement at a time, avoiding the desire to jump back and forth between different paths, even when life presents you with a multitude of opportunities. The blue jay, although diverse and inquisitive, will repeat the behavior that brings success and mastery of his environment. You are asked to do the same when this bird comes to you. Try mimicking the sounds of birds and animals as a form of playfulness and inspiration. The blue jay family loves to perform, and practicing some of their tactics will help you overcome your own sense of fear and inhibition.

# Seagull

*medicine:* adaptation, observation, going with the flow

*family:* Laridae

*diet:* as scavengers, they eat almost anything.

*Habitat:* near lakes, oceans, rivers, ponds, and urban areas

Since moving to Vancouver Island (in the middle of writing this book), I have become a huge fan of seagulls. I have gained a silent understanding of the close ties that ancient seafarers had with these coastal birds, both as navigational aids and spiritual omens. Fisherman and mariners watched the gulls closely because of their abilities to detect subtle changes in the weather, and even the distance from land. Old legends told that the souls of deceased sailors would return in the form of seagulls, making this bird a powerful omen for those tied to the ways of the waters. In medieval times, people believed that seagulls were the spirits of those who had drowned at sea. These tales become hauntingly vivid when you catch a glimpse of a seagull over the rough waters. Their bright white feathers cast an eerie glow against the dark gray skies. Seagulls have always followed ships out to sea, which would have also contributed to these wonderful sea stories.

Gulls nest in noisy, densely packed colonies and are known to have complex social structures and means of communication. Like crows and blue jays, they are highly inquisitive birds, and demonstrate a keen adaptability to their environments—even mobbing would-be predators to protect their territory. As scavengers, seagulls are naturally intelligent birds, making the best of the resources at hand. Seagulls eat trash, leftovers, and, in the case of those by the ocean, dine feverishly on crabs, mussels, and clams, dropping them from up high onto rocks below to open their tough shells. Those that dwell near people will eat anything, and have a particular fondness for french fries and potato chips.

Seagulls can be found in garbage dumps and areas where there has been a lot of urban development. They are thus symbolic of great versatility and freedom, and remind us to go with the natural flow of life. Seagull is the rebel—unique and odd and proud of it, the "patron of those inventors who are trying to find new, ingenious, and unexpected ways to do things."[26]

The seagull's connection to water makes it a harbinger of emotional healing. The diving of the seagull draws your attention to emotional wounds that may need healing. There are things that must be let go in order for any forward progress to occur. It is a time to soar above the emotions that have held you back up to this point and glide over them on the wings of the seagull spirit.

## *Connecting with Seagull Medicine*

The oceans and seas are mysterious places, filled with many varieties of life. Numerous myths center upon the water, or creatures that were believed to dwell there. Like the deep waters, our unconscious minds are filled with many strange and often frightening things. This is a totem that requires the energies of water for its greatest well being. Spend time connecting to the changing rhythms of water—from gentle

---

26. Raven Kaldera and Tannin Schwartzstein, *Urban Primitive* (Llewellyn), 229

and calm to rapid and furious. These are also the natural rhythms of our emotions, and must be recognized and put into harmony. Seagull is also an exceptional opportunist, and will teach you how to recognize a good thing when you see it. To connect with seagull medicine, become aware of all of the resources at hand. This will improve your ability to see alternate ways of looking at your world.

## Dove/Pigeon

*medicine:* peace, hope, purity, security of the home, foundation, finding your way

*family:* Columbidae

*diet:* seeds, fruit, plants

*habitat:* this family is distributed almost everywhere on earth—grasslands, savannas, tropical forest, woodlands, farms, prairie, and urban areas

Doves and pigeons are often used interchangeably in world mythologies, and carry much of the same mystical qualities. There are many species of dove and pigeon, and they vary considerably in size and habitat. This avian family has adapted to nearly every habitat on the planet, giving them a knowledgable foundation regarding the diversity of earth life. I have separated the two birds below for the purposes of their specific mythological associations. It would be wise to study the attributes of both dove and pigeon for a greater understanding of their medicine qualities if one of these birds has come to you as a totem.

## Dove

Although the dove has been viewed for centuries as a symbol of peace, its imagery dates back much further. In earlier times, particularly in ancient Greece, the dove was an emblem of sexuality and was sacred to the goddesses of love within several cultures. Although this attribute would have disappeared with the later Christian symbolism, it should be remembered that sexuality in the ancient world was looked upon as a sacred act of merging with the divine, not as something to be feared or cast aside. The dove came to represent fertility alongside the potent forces of sexual energy. It was revered among the Greeks, Egyptians, and Phoenicians, and later became the sacred bird of Bacchus in the Roman pantheon.

The ancients would often substitute the dove for a human as a sacrificial offering to the deities because of its perceived purity and innate spirituality. Dove medicine, containing the energies of sexuality, gentleness, purity, and peacefulness, is a very ancient and profound wisdom. It is the idea of union with the source of life that sexual energy and spirituality both strive to fulfill. In the ancient world, the dove was symbolic of prophecy. It was also the bird of many goddesses of the pagan world, including Venus of Rome, Ishtar of Babylon, and the Semitic Astarte. Aphrodite, who had this bird as a companion, was a goddess of sacred love as well as erotic love. In India the dove symbolized *paravata,* the symbol of lust.

As a totem bird, the dove connects us to calmness and a sense of peacefulness. They are excellent parents and embody the energies of the hearth and home. As symbols of the archetypal feminine principal, they are nurturing, compassionate, and endow their human companions with abundant creative energy. The dove totem promises a new beginning after a period of stagnation and hardship, and reminds us to be gentle with ourselves in times of great transitions.

## Pigeon

The pigeon is famous for being able to find its way back home no matter where it travels. Some scientists believe that these birds are able to detect the earth's magnetic field, which enables them to determine where they are in relation to their nest site. The pigeon has a very close relationship and sensitivity to the planet, which is a natural gift for the person who carries its medicine powers.

Pigeons have been used as messengers for thousands of years due to their homing abilities. They were utilized by the ancient Greeks, and later throughout the Roman Empire as messengers, which eventually led to their being revered among the Christians as a messenger of God.

A pigeon totem is protection in numbers, and is usually passive in conflicts with others. It is clever and witty, and "watches the city go by in all its wild and lively glory with quiet humor."[27] Pigeon is the protector and companion of those who thrive in the city by simply going with the flow, laughing at life's frustrations, and enjoying the vibrant life and rich culture to be found there. The pigeon is a hardy and tough bird, able to survive in the urban jungle. Pigeon people are generally not ambitious, and prefer to live a modest life. They do not seek fame or great wealth simply because it

---

27. Kaldera and Schwartzstein, 223.

would bring too many unwanted influences. Day-to-day living is a joy, and the small things in life are always cherished.

If a pigeon or dove appear as a totem, it may be time to return to the solitude of home. It is a message to look to the comforts of your abode for solace at this time, and to release any disharmony within the mind and body. Listen to the gentle breeze of the earth and the quiet song of the night, and reconnect with your most solid foundations upon the Earth.

### Connecting with Dove/Pigeon Medicine

As totems of familial roots, reconnecting with family members is an excellent way to understand the power of dove and pigeon. Work on creating a comforting atmosphere within your home. A space that allows you to relax and be at peace with your world will enhance your connection to your dove and pigeon totem. Like the hummingbird, connecting with the dove and pigeon totems entails the quiet appreciation of the simple life.

Some More
Fabulous Birds

Here we find some amazing birds with their own unique qualities that fit in a category all their own. As you read on, you will notice a diverse group of birds that seem to defy a solid classification in terms of attributes, but undoubtedly have much to share with humankind.

## Ostrich

*medicine:* strength, grounding ethereal knowledge

*family:* Struthionidae

*diet:* seeds, shrubs, grass, plants

*habitat:* open land, savannas, desert

The ostrich, a flightless bird, is the world's fastest two-legged animal. It definitely has a unique appearance, and I personally admire their long, flightless feathers. It is also the largest bird in the world, reaching up to eight feet tall, and weighing up to three hundred pounds. It is a very powerful bird, with enough physical strength to seriously harm, or even kill, a human. When a predator approaches, this bird becomes a master of disguise by lying flat on the ground, and giving the appearance of a lump of dirt. At other times, the ostrich will simply run away, at speeds of up to 70 mph, as they are able to detect the presence of predators from far away.

The ostrich, like the magpie, is attracted to shiny objects, and will often eat them. They are also known to eat small rocks, which helps them break down the other strange things they sometimes ingest. They are known as being able to eat almost anything, which is symbolic for an ostrich totem, who will be adept at digesting all of life's experiences, no matter how detrimental to their nature.

Ostrich eggs have been prized in many areas of the world for their strength and durability, and were often used in Egypt and Africa as vessels for carrying water. Ostrich feathers were important in ancient Egypt, and the goddess Ma'at, representing truth and justice, was usually depicted with a feather from this bird. Ma'at would weigh the souls of the dead against the ostrich feather to determine if the soul was "light" enough to ascend to the heavens of the afterlife.

As a totem, the ostrich stands as the link between the earth and the spirit worlds. Its long neck connects us to the etheric realms, but its inability to fly teaches us how to bring the knowledge of spirit down to earth for practical use. This is an important bird for those who work with a great deal of bird medicine, as the energies of flight can make one giddy and distracted, like having one's head in the clouds.

The feathers of the ostrich have been prized for thousands of years, and have adorned Egyptian Pharaohs, Roman emperors, the Black Prince, Napoleon, and Queen Victoria. In Babylonian myth, the ostrich was connected to the Dark Goddess Tiamat. The Kung Bushmen of Africa thought the ostrich had supernatural powers, and ritual ostrich dances were an integral part of their cultural expression. Ostrich feathers were considered aristocratic due to their grand appearance, and have been used in many coats of arms.

## Connecting with Ostrich Medicine

Ostrich is an Earth-bound bird, but an important ally when learning how to ground spiritual wisdom. To connect with this bird, visualize the worlds of spirit and earth merging together as one. What could you do with that kind of knowledge? Ostrich medicine is the way in which we incorporate divine knowledge into our lives on planet earth. It is the flight of the spirit coming back down to the ground. Walk in both worlds to enhance your relationship with this bird, and share the wisdom that comes forth from that union.

## Vulture/Condor

*medicine:* purification, death and rebirth

*family:* Cathartidae

*diet:* carrion

*habitat:* Andean mountains, coniferous forest, oak savannas

The Andean Condor, although not the prettiest bird in the world, is one of my favorite attractions at the Calgary Zoo, showing off his impressive 10-foot wingspan to awestruck observers. It is the largest flying bird in the Western hemisphere, and is an awesome sight to behold. The habitat of the Andean condor consists of open grasslands and mountainous areas up to 16,000 feet in elevation. The relatives of the Andean condor include the turkey vulture and the California condor, and they are all nothing short of impressive. These birds inhabit the skies at extreme heights, soaring high on thermals over the Andean Mountains, or the mountainous regions of California and the Grand Canyon. Many Peruvian shamans value the condor as a powerful healer, and its feathers are collected naturally and used for shamanic ceremonies. The condor's importance in South

America parallels that of the eagle in North American native traditions.

The vulture, or condor, carries much ancient wisdom, not only regarding death, but of the inevitable transformations that follow. Buffie Johnson explains:

> For reasons far more obvious in ancient times than they are today, the bird most recognized as the symbol of transformation was the vulture. This bird, a form of the Death Goddess, does not kill; it awaits death and transforms it. By eating the dead it performs an important function; it takes back into itself the perishable flesh, which it transmutes for rebirth.[28]

This is an important part of spiritual alchemy, although it has traditionally been symbolized by the Phoenix. In Greek mythology, the vulture was considered a descendant of the legendary Griffin. In Inca mythology, the condor represented the higher realms on the world axis, where superior beings were to be found. The condor was also worshiped for its large size, and many Inca tribes believed themselves to be descendants of these magnificent birds.

In the ancient town of Catal Huyuk, in modern-day Turkey, archaeologists uncovered a room they called the "Vuture Shrine," dating back to approximately 6500 BCE. Inside the room were images of vultures who apparently removed the heads of the human figures (probably representing removal of the soul). There were also images of human figures dressed in vulture skins.

---

28. Johnson, 95

The Goddess Ma'at of ancient Egyptian mythology was usually depicted with the wings of a vulture. She was the Goddess who symbolized the order of the world, an attribute still given to this bird around the world today. The vulture, then, is symbolic of the balance of the life and death cycles within nature.

Condor medicine is very sacred, teaching the mysteries of life and death. Its eating habits remind us that devouring the unclean and "dead" aspects of ourselves and our lives is essential to the cycle of life. It is one of those rare species that does not kill anything for its own survival, like the crow and raven. It holds a special place on earth, transmuting death into the sustenance for its own life.

Those with this condor's medicine will require a vast amount of personal space, and, like eagle medicine people, will have very lofty ideals and dreams. Those aligned with condor medicine have an innate trust in the universe, and will soar harmoniously with Great Spirit throughout their lives. Condor is the earth's purifier, ridding the world of that which no longer serves its purpose. This is a difficult aspect of this bird's medicine. Letting go of that which does not serve our path can seem impossible, even painful. You are entering a purification if condor has chosen to work with you. It is also a messenger of reaching the heights without great effort. Achieving that to which we aspire need not wear us out. When we soar with the currents of the universe, achieving becomes effortless. Conserve your energy as the condor does, and follow the rhythms of your own progress.

The vulture is a favorite bird among Buddhists because of its nature of renewing and recycling. It is symbolic of reincarnation, a process that renews the human soul with each new incarnation after death. It was believed that the fifth Dalai Lama, Losang Gyatso, could shape shift into the form of a white vulture. The ancient Greeks believed the vulture was born from the wind due to its incredible flying capabilities. They made it a symbol of union between Heaven and Earth, good and evil, spiritual and material contained within one bird image. The Pueblo Indians used vulture feathers to ground themselves, or to "come back to the self" after performing shape-shifting ceremonies.

### Connecting with Condor Medicine

Another very ancient bird totem, the condor teaches a heavy wisdom. To embrace the cycles of life and death that the condor represents, conduct a ritual intended for releasing those things that are dead in your life. Give these things away to the spirit of Condor who will transmute those things into new life. This is wonderful for releasing old emotional debris and thought patterns. Spending time in lofty places will help you understand the heightened perspective of this great bird. Visiting a mountainous region would be an extraordinary experience for anyone with a condor/vulture totem.

## Woodpecker

*medicine:* rhythm, prophecy, self discovery

*family:* Picidae

*diet:* insects, nuts, sap, fruit

*habitat:* woodlands, savannas, rainforests, bamboo forests

I used to live in a completely wooden house that towered over every other house in the neighborhood. After I moved in, I had the luxury of putting away my alarm clock, and was awakened every morning—on time—by the rhythmic hammering of a woodpecker on my roof. Most people would be annoyed, I'm sure, but not a bird watcher like me, who strained to see the culprit from the bedroom window.

The woodpecker is the earth's drummer, tapping into the rhythms of her heartbeat. This connects the woodpecker to the ancient shamanic drumming that allows the medicine man, or woman, to journey through the spirit worlds in a trance-like state. Those with woodpecker medicine tend to follow their own unique rhythms, and are often able to move in and out of other dimensions at will. Woodpecker medicine involves finding the rhythm of your life, even if it means being out of rhythm with others. This totem signals a need to "march to the beat of your own drum." If you have been going along with someone else's idea of the ideal then this is your moment to alter your course. Woodpecker wisdom is a profound look at the natural rhythms of our own bodies, minds, emotions, and thoughts.

The sound of the woodpecker heralds the beginning of the rainy season in many cultures, and the knocking sound it makes resembles martial drumming, resonating loudly through the forest. The woodpecker has traditionally been given the title of prophet because of its ability to see beyond surface layers of the trees and unearth things hidden beneath. Woodpecker teaches us how to pull back the layers of the psyche and reveal the wealth of knowledge that lies just beneath. In Roman mythology, Picus was a god of agriculture and possessed prophetic powers. He usually took the form of Mars' bird, the woodpecker. Other than *Picus,* the Romans called this bird *apiastra*; the Greeks called it *merops* (voice-possessing), *aerops* (air-voiced), or *druokolaptes* (oak-chiseler). The name *Beowulf*, contrary to popular belief, actually translates into "bee-wolf," which is another name for the woodpecker because of its tendency to follow bees. It was this bird, alongside the wolf, that nourished Romulus and Remus, the founders of Rome, and also played an important role in the augury of ancient Roman civilization.

Many experts believe that there may have been a woodpecker cult in North America and all over Europe during the Neolithic Era. Some evidence suggests the presence of a woodpecker oracle that divined the weather in the Apennines. This is not hard to believe, as the woodpecker has been called the "rainmaker" for centuries. Woodpecker as a totem heralds a time of discovery. The answers you seek are hidden below the surface and must be sought out from within.

### Connecting with Woodpecker Medicine

Essential to the medicine of woodpecker is rhythm. Start drumming ceremonies, either alone or in a drumming circle, and attune yourself with the natural rhythms that are all around you. You must look at the way you walk through your life. The woodpecker teaches you to follow your own beat, even if it means walking alone. Meditate to the sound of the drum. I find it most beneficial to listen to a pre-recorded CD, which allows for silence and privacy. This is a wonderful tool for connecting with your own rhythms and will open up the doorway to the subconscious mind, revealing your own unique path to attainment.

## Rooster/Cockerel

*medicine:* fertility, watchfulness, sexuality, pride

*family:* Phasianidae

*diet:* omnivorous

*habitat:* farmyards, prairies

The rooster is one of those birds with a very earthbound energy. As the announcer of the morning, and the source of much fertility, the rooster has a very close connection with the sun in world mythology. It was a solar emblem to the ancient Greeks because of its habit of rising every morning to greet the return of the sun. A Greek myth of the rooster tells how a youth named Alectryon (the Greek word for *rooster*) was appointed by the god Ares to stand guard while he and the goddess Aphrodite had a secret union. The youth fell asleep, and Helios, the sun, walked in on the couple. The angry god Ares turned Alectryon into a rooster, who now never forgets to announce the arrival of the sun.

In Zoroastrianism, the rooster was a symbol of protection against evil because of his watchfulness, and was representative of light and goodness. Rooster was believed to guard against evil as a close associate with the sun. The bird's role is similar in Viking myth, where one of the mythology's roosters, Vithafmir, sits atop the World Tree Yggdrasil and guards against evil. The other, Fralar, lives in Valhalla and awakens the slain heroes for their final battle. In ancient Persian mythology the rooster was a sacred bird and is associated with Bahman. He is said to have chased away the demon of darkness and summoned people to prayer and work. His association with Bahman reveals that he was symbolic of leadership and guidance toward the Good, toward Truth. It is the bird who announces the triumph of the sun over the night, and is the overthrower of the enemy. In Chinese astrology, the rooster represents physical and moral fortitude, as well as honesty and fidelity.

People with a rooster totem may be considered slightly eccentric, and will have an air of pride about them. Because of its strong sexuality, it is a symbol of fertility through the expression of male energy. The rooster fertilizes a harem of many females, all of whom he guards against intruders or predators. This bird carries much wisdom regarding the proper use of male energy, which encompasses the actions required in order for creations to take place in all areas of our lives. Dreams and ideals are connected to feminine energies, and give us the foundation for manifestation on the earth plane, but it is male energy that propels us forward into action when the timing is right. Rooster advises the direction of this primal life force into the proper channels to ensure the completion of your creation.

Being a watchful bird, the message of the rooster may also be to become more observant of what is going on around you. There may be things slipping by you unnoticed if a rooster appears as a totem.

### Connecting with Rooster Medicine

If you want to get close to rooster's power, get ready for an early start! Try waking up every morning before sunrise, allowing yourself to feel the magic that stirs at dawn. You will be amazed at how much more you will see in the very early hours of the morning; it will feel as though you had been missing out on so many things by sleeping in! As you do this, become watchful and aware of all of the creatures that busy themselves at this time of the day—this will give you a greater insight into the nature of the rooster and his special way of greeting the sun every morning.

## Turkey

*medicine:* sacrifice, transcendence, giveaway

*family:* Meleagrididae

*diet:* nuts, trees, seeds, berries, insects

*habitat:* forested areas, marshland, farmyards

The turkey has a long history with humankind. It is among the most loved and revered birds in North America and holds a special honor among the Native American tribes. The turkey is a cherished symbol of sacrifice and often walks beside those who dedicate their lives for the greater good of others. It is the totem of saints, mystics, and monks, and indicates a person who has transcended Self. The essence of the Buddha is the essence of turkey medicine, and great humanitarians like Mother Teresa and Mahatma Gandhi exuded the same selfless giving. Turkey is also symbolic of Mother Earth and her abundant harvest, and reminds us that we will always have nourishment when we trust in universal abundance.

Wild turkeys are very intelligent, alert, and possess excellent survival skills. They are naturally cautious, which makes them difficult to hunt in the wild. They were given the name

"Earth-Eagle" by some tribes because of their close connection to Mother Earth, and their ability to utilize her gifts wisely. It is the give-away bird, allowing others to nourish themselves by giving up its own life. Few people ever aspire to such a feat.

Turkey medicine is a gentle reminder to give thanks to Mother Earth and the Great Spirit for the bounty we have in our lives. It is about accepting the gifts we receive with gratitude, and sharing those gifts with others—whether material, spiritual, or intellectual. If the turkey has come to you as a totem, you are being asked to strengthen your sense of compassion as well as that of gratitude. These are often the hardest lessons for people to learn, and will often take many lifetimes to perfect.

## Connecting with Turkey Medicine

If turkey comes calling to you, it is time for a give-away. Empty out the closets and donate what you *really* do not need to charity. Look beyond yourself and toward the needs of others to embrace the wisdom of the turkey. Start a gratitude journal. Take time every day to write down the things you receive or experience that instill a sense of gratitude. You will be amazed at just how much you have in comparison with many others who go without, and come to realize that you achieve nothing on your own. The spirit of turkey will also show you how to connect with the powers of creation.

# Grouse

*medicine:* rhythm, movement, sacred dance

*family:* Phasianidae

*diet:* mainly vegetation, such as buds, leaves, and twigs

*habitat:* hardwood bush and forest

Grouse are heavily built birds, especially adapted for winter weather. Their feather coloring is distinct, but their deliberate pace makes them virtually invisible within the dense forests that they inhabit. The mating dance of the grouse is perhaps one of its most distinguishing features, resembling a ceremonial dance of the distant past. It has often been connected with the Sufi dancers, or "Whirling Dervishes," whose spinning dance enables them to transcend higher levels of self-awareness.

The medicine of grouse involves working with rhythm, sacred dance, and drumming. It heralds a time of new rhythms and movements, and awakens the primal energies of dance. Drumming and dance have been performed since the beginnings of human civilization as sacred rituals, invocations, and healing ceremonies. To the Native American Indians the grouse is the keeper of the sacred spiral. The spiral has appeared all over the world as a representation of the movement of the life force, or of consciousness itself. The spiral dance actually performed by the grouse is used as a part of the courtship process, and symbolically indicates the act of moving inward toward the center. It is a powerful way of attaining inner awareness and is mimicked by many shamanic dancers. Symbolically, dancing in a circle mimics the act of creation, and the grouse as a spirit companion will show you how to *dance* new things into your experience by tapping into the natural rhythms of the universe.

If grouse appears to you as a spirit guide, look at the movement in your life and determine whether it is in tune with the natural rhythms of your heart and soul. If not, call upon the grouse to help create a life-dance that reflects your truest desires and dreams.

### Connecting with Grouse Medicine

Dancing is the most effective way to connect with the grouse's teaching. Observe their circular movements and imitate the spiral through your own body. These movements mimic the act of creation in the universe as a constant whirling mass of energy. Watch how these dances initiate your own inner sense of power, and your ability to create every day of your life. Drumming will enhance this very primal experience, but you can listen to a pre-recorded CD just as well.

8

Giving Thanks,
Giving Back

*We have enslaved the rest of the animal creation,*
*and have treated our distant cousins in fur and feather*
*so badly that beyond doubt if they were able to*
*formulate a religion, they would depict the*
*devil in human form.*

—W. R. INGR

At this point in the book I trust you can see how important birds have been to the human race and its many cultures, religions, and social structures. Now, more than ever, birds need our attention if they are going to survive our increasing technological age. The truth of the matter is that we would be in a sorry state without them. We would be overrun with crop-destroying rodents without owls and hawks. We would be mobbed with billions of insects without songbirds, and without hummingbirds, we would lose one of nature's greatest pollinators. Without naming each bird, you can surely see the disastrous ecological effects of an earth without birds, and yet, many people never give it a second thought.

I have personally seen owls, hawks, and eagles that have been killed by speeding traffic, creatures once admired, even worshipped, left to die on the side of the road. It is a sad truth, but a truth that must be heard. The magic of life on

Earth seems to wane with every passing generation. The modern world may not be as enchanting as it once was, but it can be saved. The birds, and all of Earth's animal forms that remain today, never cease in their willingness to share the secrets and wisdom of the universe. This knowledge is even more important in the present era than it ever was in the ancient world because of the devastating effects of modernization. I hope this book not only increases your appreciation for birds everywhere, but encourages you to lend your support in any way you can. Here are some things we can all do to keep our winged companions safe on the planet, and connect with their energies every day.

## Feed Your Feathered Friends

This is the easiest way to express your compassion for the avian world. Once you know what birds are native to your area, trying to get them to your yard becomes a wonderful endeavor. I used to wade through many feet of freshly fallen Alberta snow to ensure the songbirds could get to their seed. The reward of watching and listening to dozens of birds get enough to eat in bad weather is an inherent joy for me.

Make sure you know what each bird eats, and provide several different feeding stations and sources of clean water. Put up nesting houses for birds during the winter months, and keep fresh food and water supplies out all year round. You can even purchase electric bird baths that keep water from freezing outdoors in cold temperatures. Each bird will also have requirements unique to its behavioral and dietary needs, so do your research. Hummingbirds, for example, will need the nectar that comes from certain types of flowers, or from a homemade mixture of sugar and water. They are also very territorial and will not share a feeder with hummingbirds outside of their territory. Members of the finch family love thistle seeds and sunflower seeds, while the blue jay will travel anywhere for fresh peanuts and bread. Crows and magpies love cooked pasta, french fries, potato chips, dog food, hamburgers, and hot dogs, and are the perfect recipients for daily leftovers to. If you have berry bushes, keep an eye out for the waxwings, who will strip them clean in no time.

I learned many of these unique habits and tastes of birds through avid observation and experimentation, which was just as entertaining and uplifting as it was educational. There were many days when my back yard was occupied by a whole milieu of birds, including (simultaneously) crows, magpies, grackles, blue jays, woodpeckers, pine siskins, house finches, robins, and cedar waxwings. I almost needed traffic lights out there to avoid mid-aircollisions! If you are consistent with your feeding, they will return, on time, every day to see what's on the menu. These simple activities will help you connect with birds in general, even though they may not be your specific bird totem. It will also give you the chance to observe birds up close, which will naturally increase your appreciation for winged life and their unique survival skills and personalities.

Another important thing to remember is that birds in the modern world face a great many dangers caused by advances in human civilization. Many birds are hit by traffic, killed by flying into windows, or killed by domestic animals like dogs and cats. You can do very simple things to help birds avoid these dangers. Put decals on your windows so birds can identify the glass as a solid object, particularly where windows face each other, and keep cats and dogs away from active bird feeding areas to avoid conflict.

Finally, if you see a bird that has been hit by a car, or injured in some other way, contact a local wildlife rehabilitation center immediately. Your quick action could save a bird's life and allow it a safe return into the wild. Carry an emergency phone number just in case. If you happen to find a bird who has been killed, and are not comfortable picking it up, move it away from the road so that other animals and scavenger birds can nourish themselves without the risk of being hit themselves. Most of the birds that are hit by cars on highways are eagles, owls, hawks, crows, and magpies. I myself have picked up many of these birds, and have obtained the necessary permits to possess them legally according to provincial fish and wildlife laws. If you would like to do more, most wildlife rehabilitation centers are in desperate need of volunteers, both at their facilities and as rescue drivers.

## Some Bird Organizations Around the World

Birds do so much for the planet. They control the insect and rodent populations, pollinate plants, and scavenge waste. Healthy bird populations indicate healthy habitats for all species, including that of humans. If the birds are in trouble, then so is everything else within that ecosystem. Sadly, this has not been a concept readily understood by human populations who, without a doubt, are the sole reason for the loss of bird life on the planet. Birds, and all animals, have suffered from the human species, sometimes to extinction, and now face new threats of habitat changes due to atmospheric alterations. The earth needs bird life, and we can help to sustain it. Contact any one of these organizations for more information about bird conservation and find those within your specific geographical location.

## Canada

### Alberta Birds of Prey Foundation
Coaldale, Alberta
www.burrowingowl.com

### Alberta Institute for Wildlife Conservation
Madden, Alberta
www.aiwc.moonfruit.com

### Boreal Center For Bird Conservation
Slave Lake, Alberta
www.borealbirdcentre.com

### le Nichoir—Wild Bird Rehabilitation
Hudson, Quebec
www.lenichoir.org

### WWF Canada
www.wwf.ca

## U.S

### The Feather Distribution Project

Jonathan E. Reyman, Ph.D

Illinois State Museum Research and Collections Center

Springfield, Ilinois

www.wingwise.com

(collects and donates naturally molted feathers to the Pueblo
  Indians for religious and ceremonial use)

### California Raptor Center

California

www.vetmed.ucdavis.edu

### The Center for Birds of Prey

Charleston, South Carolina

www.thecenterforbirdsofprey.org

### Wild Bird Rehabilitation

St. Louis, Missouri

www.wildbirdrehab.org

### Bird Rescue Center

Santa Rosa, California

www.birdrescuecenter.org

Bibliography

Andrews, Ted. *Animal Speak: The Spiritual and Magical Powers of Creatures Great and Small.* St. Paul, MN: Llewellyn Worldwide, 1993.

Baring, Ann, and Jules Cashford. *The Myth of the Goddess: Evolution of an Image.* New York: Penguin, 1993.

Benson, Elizabeth P. *Birds and Beasts of Ancient Latin America.* Gainesville, FL: University Press of Florida, 1997.

Bierhorst, John. *The Mythology of North America.* New York: Morrow, 1985.

Bonnefoy, Yves, and Wendy Doniger. *Asian Mythologies.* Chicago: University of Chicago Press, 1993.

Bradley, Ian C. *The Celtic Way.* London: Darton Longman & Todd Ltd., 2003.

Brehm, Alfred Edmund, Henry Matthew Labouchere, and William Jesse. *Bird-life: Being a History of the Bird, Its Structure, and Habits, Together with Sketches of Fifty Different Species.* J. Van Voorst, 1874.

Campbell, Joseph. *The Hero With a Thousand Faces.* New World Library, 2008.

Carr-Gomm, Philip, and Bill Worthington. *The Druid Animal Oracle: Working with the Sacred Animals of the Druid Tradition.* Connections, 1996.

Churchward, James. *The Sacred Symbols of Mu.* Charleston, SC: Forgotten Books, 1993.

Conway, D. J. *Animal Magick: The Art of Recognizing and Working with Familiars.* St. Paul, MN: Llewellyn Worldwide, 1995.

Cowan, Tom. *Fire in the Head: Shamanism and the Celtic Spirit.* New York: Harper Collins Publishers, 1993.

Cunningham, Scott. *Divination for Beginners: Reading the Past, Present and Future.* St. Paul, MN: Llewellyn Worldwide, 2003.

Dimmitt, Cornelia, and Johannes Adrianus Bernardus Buitenen. *Classical Hindu Mythology: A Reader in the Sanskrit Puranas.* Philadelphia: Temple University Press, 1978.

Eason, Cassandra. *Fabulous Creatures, Mythical Monstors, and Animal Power Symbols: A Handbook.* Oxford, UK: Greenwood Publishing Group, 2007.

Fienup-Riordan, Ann. *Boundaries and Passages: Rule and Ritual in Yup'ik Eskimo Oral Tradition.* Norman, OK: University of Oklahoma Press, 1995.

Franklin, Anna. *Oracle of the Goddess.* NP: Vega Books, 2003.

Gimbutas, Marija. *The Living Goddesses.* Berkeley, CA: University of California Press, 2001.

Greene, Rosalyn. *The Magic of Shapeshifting.* Newburyport, MA: Weiser, 2000.

Greene, Thomas M. *Poetry, Signs and Magic.* Newark, DE: University of Delaware Press, 2005.

Grimassi, Raven. *The Witch's Familiar: Spiritual Partnerships for Successful Magic.* St. Paul, MN: Llewellyn Worldwide, 2003.

Heinz, Sabine. *Celtic Symbols.* New York: Sterling Publishing Company, Inc., 2008.

Johnson, Buffie. *Lady of the Beasts: the Goddess and Her Sacred Animals.* Rochester, VT: Inner Traditions, 1994.

Kaldera, Raven, and Tannin Schwartzstein, *The Urban Primitive.* St. Paul, MN: Llewellyn Worldwide, 2002.

King, Scott Alexander. *Animal Dreaming: the Spiritual and Symbolic Language of the Australasian Animals.* Glen Waverly, AU: Blue Angel Gallery, 2007.

Knight, Richard Payne, and Alexander Wilder. *The Symbolical Language and Mythology: An Inquiry.* New York: J. W. Bouton, 1876.

Krech, Shepard, and Shepard Krech III. *Spirits of the Air: Birds and American Indians in the South.* Athens, GA: University of Georgia Press, 2009.

Institute of Ethnic Literature, CASS. 2003–2009.

Laubin, Reginald. *Indian Dances of North America: Their Importance to Indian Life.* Norman, OK: University of Oklahoma Press, 1989.

Laufer, Berthold. *Bird Divination Among the Tibetans.* VDM Verlag Dr. Muller Edition Classic.

Lundberg, Murray, from his article "The Spiritual Swan," 2003-2009.

MacKay, Barry Kent. *Bird Sounds: How and Why Birds Sing, Call, Chatter, and Screech.* Mechanicsburg, PA: Stackpole Books, 2001.

Matthews, John, and Ari Beck. *Celtic Totem Animals.* Newburyport, MA: Red Wheel, 2002.

Meletinsky, Eleazar M., Guy Lanoue, and Alexandre Sadetsky. *The Poetics of Myth.* London: Routledge, 2000.

Mickaharic, Draja. *Magical Techniques.* Bloomington, IN: Xlibris Corporation, 2002.

Milne, Courtney, and Sherrill Miller. *Visions of the Goddess.* New York: Penguin Studio, 1998.

Mooney, James. *Myths of the Cherokee and Sacred Formulas of the Cherokees.* Nashville, TN: Charles and Randy Elder-Booksellers, 1982.

Nozedar, Adele. *The Secret Language of Birds: A Spiritual Treasury of Myths, Folklore and Inspirational True Stories.* New York: HarperCollins Publishers Limited, 2006.

Payam, Nabarz. *The Mysteries of Mithras: the Pagan Belief that Shaped the Christian World.* Rochester, VT: Inner Traditions/Bear & Company, 2005.

Rodriguez, Junius P. *Encyclopedia of Slave Resistance and Rebellion.* Oxford, UK: Greenwood Pub. Group, 2007.

Savage, Candace. *Crows: Encounters With the Wise Guys of the Avian World.* Vancouver, BC: Greystone Books, 2007.

Savage, Candace. *Peregrine Falcons.* Vancouver, BC: Douglas & McIntyre, 1992.

Sax, Boria. *The Mythical Zoo: An Encyclopedia of Animals in World Myth, Legend, and Literature.* ABC-CLIO, 2001.

Spence, Lewis. *Myths and Legends of the North American Indians.* Vancouver, BC: Kessinger Publishing, 1997.

*The Book of Gems.* Cambridge, MA: Harvard University, 1846.

Turner, Patricia, and Charles Russell Coulter. *Dictionary of Ancient Deities.* New York: Oxford University Press US, 2001.

Welch, Patricia Bjaaland. *Chinese Art: A Guide to Motifs and Visual Imagery.* Boston: Tuttle Publishing, 2008.

Werness, Hope B., Joanne H. Benedict, Scott Thomas, and Tiffany Ramsay-Lozano. *The Continnum Encyclopedia of Animal Symbolism in Art.* New York: Continuum International Publishing Group, 2004.

Williams, Charles Alfred Speed, and Terence Barrow. *Chinese Symbolism and Art Motifs: A Comprehensive Handbook on Symbolism in Chinese Art Through the Ages.* Boston: Tuttle Publishing, 2006.

*World Mythology.* London: Parragon Publishing, 2003.